The Wealth Guide

THE *FINANCIAL TIMES'* GUIDE TO MANAGING YOUR MONEY

PENGUIN BOOKS

in association with the Financial Times

PENGUIN BOOKS

Published by the Penguin Group
Penguin Books Ltd, 27 Wrights Lane, London w8 5TZ, England
Penguin Putnam Inc., 375 Hudson Street, New York, New York 10014, USA
Penguin Books Australia Ltd, Ringwood, Victoria, Australia
Penguin Books Canada Ltd, 10 Alcorn Avenue, Toronto, Ontario, Canada M4V 3B2
Penguin Books (NZ) Ltd, Private Bag 102902, NSMC, Auckland, New Zealand

Penguin Books Ltd, Registered Offices: Harmondsworth, Middlesex, England

First published by the *Financial Times* as *The Wealth Course* 1998
This edition published in Penguin Books, 1999
10 9 8 7 6 5 4 3 2 1

Written by Barry Riley, Philip Loggan, Gillian O'Connor, Jean Eaglesham and Debbie Harrison

Graphics Paul Slater and Nigel Andrews

Editor Gillian O'Connor

With thanks to Simon London

Cartoons by Roger Beale

Set in 11/14 pt PostScript Adobe Minion
Typeset by Rowland Phototypesetting Ltd, Bury St Edmunds, Suffolk
Printed in England by Clays Ltd, St Ives plc

CONTENTS

This series of articles, first published in the *Financial Times*, introduces readers to the investment theories and techniques used by professional investors such as Warren Buffett and George Soros. It has been written by the *Financial Times'* own experts, such as Barry Riley, investment editor, and Philip Coggan, markets editor. Anyone reading these pieces should gain a clear idea of how investment markets work, and how to make them work for him or her.

The introductory articles are designed to help readers identify their investment needs and objectives. These vary, depending on age, income and other financial and family circumstances. We also explain how to choose a financial adviser or stockbroker.

The main part of the book is a guide to the investment universe and how you can make money there. The classifications are easy enough: most investments are made up of equities, fixed-interest stocks, property and cash. But which combinations work best? Can you avoid investing just before markets collapse? And should you be looking for value or growth? These are just some of the topics covered.

Many people nowadays put their money into packaged products, such as unit trusts, life assurance and pensions. These contain the same ingredients, but it can be difficult to see inside the package. So we conclude by analysing what is on offer, and how to choose the right products for you.

The *Financial Times* contains plenty of information which can help you make these choices, and the book will highlight those parts of the newspaper relevant to the subject being discussed.

Consider the wider picture first

Successful professional investors are like successful generals: they have realistic objectives and a clear strategy. Private investors need investment strategies too. But first you have to consider what your objectives are

'The market, like the Lord, helps those who help themselves.'

Warren Buffett, the patron saint of private investors, does not believe in gambling. He believes in hard work, understanding what you are buying and never taking unnecessary risks.

Not all successful professional investors use the same strategies as Buffett. But, though their strategies differ, they all have strategies. They know what they want their investments to achieve. And they are usually very clear about how they pick shares and manage their portfolios in order to achieve their objectives.

Private investors can learn some useful techniques from the pros. But, unlike a professional investment manager, they also need to decide where their investment portfolios fit into their wider personal finances.

● **First things first.** Anyone considering investing on the stock market should check that all their other financial defences are already in place: house, pension, emergency cash fund and the relevant life and protection cover. It is stupid to buy long-term securities, such as shares, if they may have to be cashed in prematurely to meet everyday bills or a crisis.

Life assurance is only necessary if you have dependants who will suffer financially if you die. Many employers provide it automatically as part of the company pension scheme. Insurance against permanent and critical illness – leaving you unable to work – is advisable even for single people.

Making sure you will have an adequate pension, or an alternative

2

source of income in retirement, is essential. Companies are increasingly moving away from expensive schemes where the pension is linked to employees' final salary. And few people nowadays stay in one job long enough to collect the benefits of a lifetime's service. Although there are other ways of accumulating wealth to live off in your later years, such as building up a business, the tax concessions enjoyed by pension schemes make it foolish to ignore them. It is an industry truism that most people leave it too late to start worrying about their pension.

• **What are your investment objectives?** Once you have all your safety nets in place, set down what you want your investments to do for you over what period of time. Some people have a very specific objective, such as paying for their children's school fees or providing a supplementary pension for themselves. A lucky minority can afford to treat their investments as a hobby, knowing that all their basic financial needs are already well provided for.

Some age-based generalizations are useful as a starting point. An investor's age often determines the period over which they invest. Thus, younger people are usually at the stage where they are trying to accumulate wealth, and can work to a timescale of several decades. As a result, they can normally afford to invest for capital growth rather than income, and to take some risks with their money.

Older people, often working to a shorter timescale, will usually be more cautious, and they may need to rely on the income from their investments to meet their day-to-day bills.

But few people fit a stereotype exactly. What's more, people's lives are both messier and less predictable than they used to be. They get divorced, change jobs or are made redundant. Can you safely predict what your circumstances will be in ten years' time? Although it is sensible to have a broad financial plan, it is also necessary to have one that is flexible enough to accommodate the unexpected. And, although it is sensible to have definite investment objectives, it is dangerous to tie yourself into a strategy which could be disastrous if your circumstances change.

Your character will also influence your investment strategy. Some people are naturally cautious, some naturally adventurous. Trying to temper a natural bias is often worthwhile. Most people are too cautious for their own financial good – but adopting a strategy you feel uncomfortable with could well cause problems further down the road. If, say, you have an equity portfolio, you must have the mental stamina to watch your shares dip below their purchase cost without rushing for the exit. Cautious people may well choose investment strategies suitable for older people. That may mean they end life poorer, but that's the price of peace of mind.

• **How much risk can you accept?** This is really an elaboration of the last point. Investments offer a hierarchy of risk. Cash offers low risk and low rewards, fixed interest medium risk and medium rewards, equities high risk and high rewards, and some types of equity or highly geared investment very high risks and potentially very high rewards. If you are young and carefree you will aim high, old and cautious and you will aim low.

• **How much money do you have?** The amount of money you can afford affects your strategy in two ways. If you do not have much spare cash, you may be more cautious. But people without much money also have a restricted choice of investments.

For example, the costs of buying individual shares may be excessive, and you may not be able to afford to buy shares in more than one or two companies, which is riskier than buying several. So the only sensible choice may be to invest through a pooled fund, such as a unit trust.

• **What is the market climate like?** Stock market investment is a long-term business, and trying to get your money in at the bottom and out at the top is virtually impossible. But that does not mean you can afford to ignore market conditions. Anyone who put a large sum of money into equities in early October 1987 – or in July 1998 – had time to repent at leisure.

Private investors will find it expensive to chop and change their portfolios frequently. But there is certainly no reason to put new money into the market if you are convinced it will fall in the short term.

Anyone investing a lump sum at any stage of their life should adopt a relatively cautious strategy. If, say, you were originally planning on an 80/20 equity/bonds split, consider making it 70/30. And invest the money gradually, over at least a year. Park the majority in a safe short-term, high-interest deposit account, and build up your investment portfolio over a period.

SO YOU WANT TO BE AN INVESTOR?

4

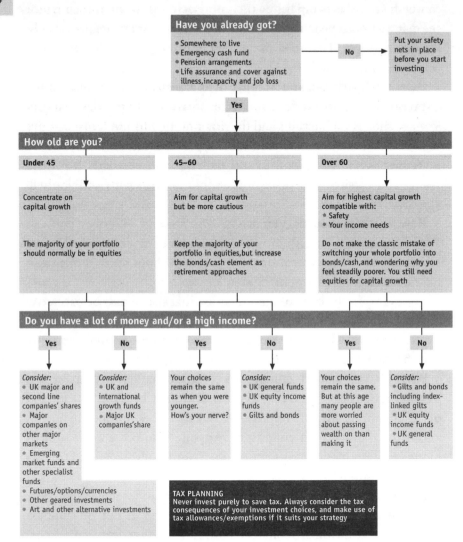

Have you already got?
- Somewhere to live
- Emergency cash fund
- Pension arrangements
- Life assurance and cover against illness, incapacity and job loss

No → Put your safety nets in place before you start investing

Yes

How old are you?

Under 45	45–60	Over 60
Concentrate on capital growth	Aim for capital growth but be more cautious	Aim for highest capital growth compatible with: • Safety • Your income needs
The majority of your portfolio should normally be in equities	Keep the majority of your portfolio in equities, but increase the bonds/cash element as retirement approaches	Do not make the classic mistake of switching your whole portfolio into bonds/cash, and wondering why you feel steadily poorer. You still need equities for capital growth

Do you have a lot of money and/or a high income?

Yes	No	Yes	No	Yes	No
Consider: • UK major and second line companies' shares • Major companies on other major markets • Emerging market funds and other specialist funds • Futures/options/currencies • Other geared investments • Art and other alternative investments	*Consider:* • UK and international growth funds • Major UK companies' share	Your choices remain the same as when you were younger. How's your nerve?	*Consider:* • UK general funds • UK equity income funds • Gilts and bonds	Your choices remain the same. But at this age many people are more worried about passing wealth on than making it	*Consider:* • Gilts and bonds including index-linked gilts • UK equity income funds • UK general funds

TAX PLANNING
Never invest purely to save tax. Always consider the tax consequences of your investment choices, and make use of tax allowances/exemptions if it suits your strategy

● **What about tax?** Investing in anything simply because of the tax breaks attached to it is usually a good way of losing money. Governments grant tax concessions to schemes such as venture capital trusts because they want to attract money into activities which are not usually considered good risks. And the additional costs of tax shelters often cancel out the tax advantages.

But it is sensible to take advantage of all the standard tax concessions if you can do so easily. If, for example, one partner in a marriage expects to make a lot of capital gains and the other none, why not transfer some securities across, so that both can take advantage of the annual capital gains tax allowance? If you intend to have an investment portfolio anyway, it is prudent to shelter some of it inside an individual savings account, although the tax benefits are on the wane. If you want to buy gilts, buy those which are most tax-efficient.

● **Which bits of your investment do you want to do yourself?** You need to have an investment strategy, but you do not need to run your portfolio yourself unless you want to. People without the time or interest should concentrate their efforts on picking a good adviser or manager. And even those who do have the time and interest should probably have the bulk of their money under professional management until they have found out if they are any good at investing.

HOW THE FT CAN HELP

Deposit accounts

Your cash is part of your portfolio, and it is important to earn the best return on it. But finding the right place to park it can be difficult because investors have so much choice. Every Saturday, Weekend Money has a list of **best deposit rates** to help you pick a suitable place. The right home for your money depends on a number of factors.

First, though, do distinguish between cash which is part of your long-term investment portfolio, and the cash in your current account. Most current accounts are subject to heavy traffic in and out, as your monthly pay cheque is whittled away by your regular spending. This is costly for the firm running the account. So do not expect to get top rates of interest on a current account, and do transfer excess funds to a savings account.

■ **Best deposit rates**

Always remember to consider your own tax status when deciding which is the best for you. A new rates tables is best rates for the new generation of Tessas. If you have a maturing Tessa, you hav decide whether to reinvest your capital for a further five years in a new Tessa. The table lists s currently available for "Tessa Twos".

Instant Access Accounts	Telephone	Account	Notice or term	Deposit
Nationwide BS	0500 302010	InvestDirect	Postal	£1
C&G	0800 742437	Instant Transfer	Instant (T)	£1,000
Safeway	0800 995995	Direct Savings	Instant (B)	£2,500
SAGA (for over 50s)	0800 300555	Postal Savings	Postal	£10,000
Notice accounts & bonds				
Chelsea BS	0800 132351	Post-tel 40	40 Day (B)	£5,000
Standard Life Bank	0345 555657	50 Day Notice	50 Day (T)	£1
Legal & General Bank	0500 111200	90 Direct	90 Day (B)	£10,000
	0800 136605	2 year Bond	2 Years	£2,000
Monthly interest				
C&G	0800 748437	Instant Transfer	Instant (T)	£5,000

Our table categorizes savings accounts according to several different criteria. First the **term** – the period for which your money is locked up, or where there may be a financial penalty if you ask for it back prematurely. The difference between 'instant access' and 'notice' accounts – where you have to give a certain number of days' notice of withdrawals may seem obvious. But many allegedly 'instant' accounts do not offer same-day withdrawal. So use the contact numbers in the table to check out the details.

Textbooks often suggest that the longer the savings period, the higher the rate of interest. But the reverse will probably be true if interest rates are expected to fall. Some types of deposit, such as conventional guaranteed income bonds, after a fixed interest rate right through the term – handy if you are expecting a very large drop in rates over the next few years. But most are variable. Again, the table shows which do what.

The **amount** of money you are depositing also affects the rate of interest you get. Our table lists the best rates for different-sized deposits in each category. But we cannot list all sizes of deposits. So again, it is worth using the contact numbers to find out what you will get on the money you have available.

Another point to check is whether the income on the account is paid

monthly or **annually**. The table has a column which shows this. A retired person living on investment income may well want income monthly, but rates will often be slightly lower because of the administrative hassle involved. Several National Savings products offer no interest during the period of the investment: it is rolled up and paid when the investment matures. So these are wholly unsuitable for anyone needing a regular income.

Tax is another key factor to consider. Both the ISAs and the National Savings Certificates listed in our table are tax-free. So the interest rates they offer cannot be directly compared with others in the table. Remember that tax-free accounts normally offer the best value to people paying high rates of tax.

Two final points.

● Our table offers some yardsticks. But it will not suit all savers. So shop around.

● Many savings accounts offering attractive rates have strings and limitations which diminish their attractions. So look before you leap.

TOP TIP

Life cover

Life assurance is cheap and readily available. How much do you need?

1. Do you have any dependants? Do you have a wife/husband/ partner who would suffer financially if you died? Do you have young children/elderly parents/others who rely on you? If you answered 'No' to these questions, you do not need life assurance.

If you answered 'Yes' to any of them, read on.

2. Rule of thumb. If you have a dependent partner but no children, reckon on term assurance for four times your annual salary plus your net debts. (For example, if you earn £100,000 a year you need cover of £400,000, plus, say, £200,000 for the mortgage.)

If you also have a couple of children, cover yourself for ten times your salary. (For example, if you earn £100,000 and have a £200,000 mortgage, reckon on cover of £1.2m.)

Advisers often recommend ordinary term life assurance, where you can pay as little as £5 a month for every £100,000 of cover. If you die, this provides a lump sum which can be used to pay off debts, with the remainder invested to produce a regular income for your dependants.

An alternative for the latter job is family income benefit, a form of term assurance which provides an annual income for a certain period of years (e.g. until the last child will leave university). Some versions provide increasing payouts to cope with inflation.

Advisers also counsel against buying complex products, such as whole-of-life policies, which combine savings with protection. They tend to be both inflexible and expensive. So keep your protection policies and your savings plans separate.

PS. Many companies provide some free life cover for employees as part of the company pension scheme. Check before deciding whether you need to buy extra protection yourself.

Wage earners are not the only ones to consider. Do remember looking after the children. Nannies are not cheap.

First steps: capital growth or steady income

Your investment choice depends on whether you want your savings to increase or to provide you with regular returns

The division between capital and income, and the sanctity of capital, is a cliché. And, like most clichés, it is useful up to a point.

As pointed out in the last article, younger investors are normally seeking to accumulate wealth and will be primarily interested in capital growth. By contrast, older investors often rely on the income from their investments to finance some of their everyday spending, and will want that income to be as high as possible.

But the great divide ignores two important points. First, inflation can substantially erode the purchasing power of capital. So today even income seekers need to preserve the real (inflation-adjusted) value of their capital. Second, the divide itself is, in many ways, a fiction.

● **Look at the total return.** The yardstick professional investors use when sizing up investments is total return, which includes both capital growth and income. Personal investors should do the same, for focusing solely on growth or income can produce at best a partial, at worst a misleading, picture. This is partly because some investments are skewed to accentuate one or the other aspect.

Thus zero-dividend bonds and gilt strips produce no income as such, but the capital gain over the holding period compensates for this and the total return is comparable to those on other fixed-interest stocks.

By contrast, a few gilts offer an abnormally high interest (running) yield. But in this case the market price is substantially above the price at which the stock will eventually be bought back by the government,

THE GREAT DIVIDE

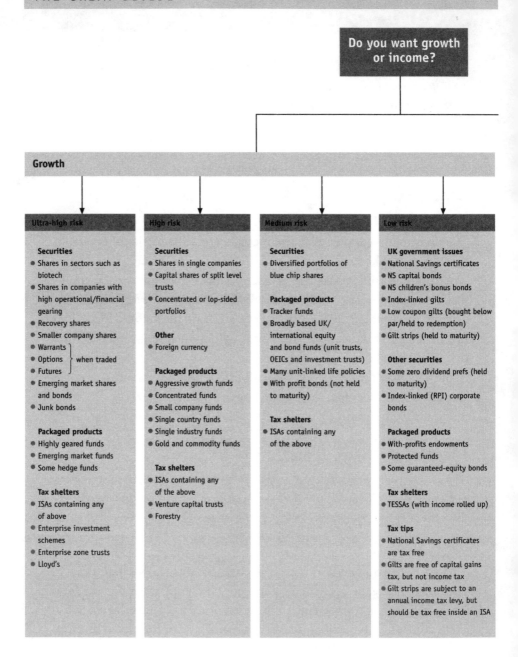

Do you want growth or income?

Growth

Ultra-high risk

Securities
- Shares in sectors such as biotech
- Shares in companies with high operational/financial gearing
- Recovery shares
- Smaller company shares
- Warrants ⎤
- Options ⎬ when traded
- Futures ⎦
- Emerging market shares and bonds
- Junk bonds

Packaged products
- Highly geared funds
- Emerging market funds
- Some hedge funds

Tax shelters
- ISAs containing any of above
- Enterprise investment schemes
- Enterprise zone trusts
- Lloyd's

High risk

Securities
- Shares in single companies
- Capital shares of split level trusts
- Concentrated or lop-sided portfolios

Other
- Foreign currency

Packaged products
- Aggressive growth funds
- Concentrated funds
- Small company funds
- Single country funds
- Single industry funds
- Gold and commodity funds

Tax shelters
- ISAs containing any of the above
- Venture capital trusts
- Forestry

Medium risk

Securities
- Diversified portfolios of blue chip shares

Packaged products
- Tracker funds
- Broadly based UK/ international equity and bond funds (unit trusts, OEICs and investment trusts)
- Many unit-linked life policies
- With profit bonds (not held to maturity)

Tax shelters
- ISAs containing any of the above

Low risk

UK government issues
- National Savings certificates
- NS capital bonds
- NS children's bonus bonds
- Index-linked gilts
- Low coupon gilts (bought below par/held to redemption)
- Gilt strips (held to maturity)

Other securities
- Some zero dividend prefs (held to maturity)
- Index-linked (RPI) corporate bonds

Packaged products
- With-profits endowments
- Protected funds
- Some guaranteed-equity bonds

Tax shelters
- TESSAs (with income rolled up)

Tax tips
- National Savings certificates are tax free
- Gilts are free of capital gains tax, but not income tax
- Gilt strips are subject to an annual income tax levy, but should be tax free inside an ISA

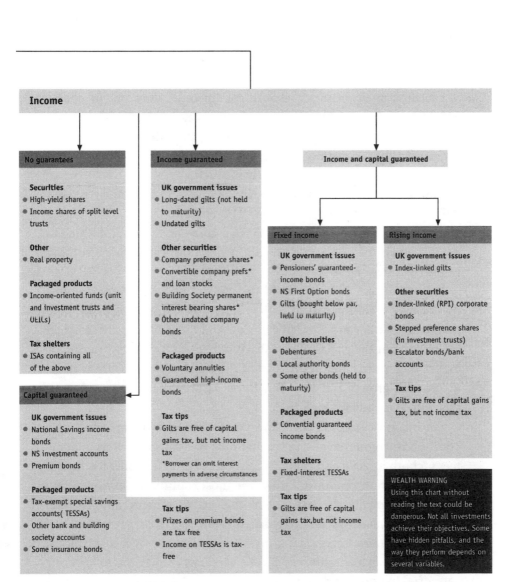

Income

No guarantees

Securities
- High-yield shares
- Income shares of split level trusts

Other
- Real property

Packaged products
- Income-oriented funds (unit and investment trusts and OEICs)

Tax shelters
- ISAs containing all of the above

Capital guaranteed

UK government issues
- National Savings income bonds
- NS investment accounts
- Premium bonds

Packaged products
- Tax-exempt special savings accounts(TESSAs)
- Other bank and building society accounts
- Some insurance bonds

Income guaranteed

UK government issues
- Long-dated gilts (not held to maturity)
- Undated gilts

Other securities
- Company preference shares*
- Convertible company prefs* and loan stocks
- Building Society permanent interest bearing shares*
- Other undated company bonds

Packaged products
- Voluntary annuities
- Guaranteed high-income bonds

Tax tips
- Gilts are free of capital gains tax, but not income tax
*Borrower can omit interest payments in adverse circumstances

Tax tips
- Prizes on premium bonds are tax free
- Income on TESSAs is tax-free

Income and capital guaranteed

Fixed income

UK government issues
- Pensioners' guaranteed-income bonds
- NS First Option bonds
- Gilts (bought below par, held to maturity)

Other securities
- Debentures
- Local authority bonds
- Some other bonds (held to maturity)

Packaged products
- Convential guaranteed income bonds

Tax shelters
- Fixed-interest TESSAs

Tax tips
- Gilts are free of capital gains tax, but not income tax

Rising income

UK government issues
- Index-linked gilts

Other securities
- Index-linked (RPI) corporate bonds
- Stepped preference shares (in investment trusts)
- Escalator bonds/bank accounts

Tax tips
- Gilts are free of capital gains tax, but not income tax

WEALTH WARNING
Using this chart without reading the text could be dangerous. Not all investments achieve their objectives. Some have hidden pitfalls, and the way they perform depends on several variables.

making a capital loss inevitable for anyone who holds to redemption. And again the total return will be in line with those on other gilts.

Many other investments offering ultra-high yields also do so by eroding the capital. And this is often less easy to spot than it is in the gilts market.

Contrariwise, any growth investor needs to look twice at funds promising to match the capital growth in a stockmarket index. For a large part of the total return from equities comes from reinvesting the income.

Labelling an investment 'growth' or 'income' does not of course ensure that it behaves appropriately. Until recently, many high yielding equity funds produced better capital growth than those with a growth tag. And funds targeting capital growth, such as emerging market funds, have often come spectacularly unstuck.

● **How to use our chart.** Most private investors want their returns delivered in the appropriate form. The chart on pages 10–11 shows which investments are generally sold to income investors, and which to growth investors. We have then subdivided both categories according to the risk tolerances of investors.

If, say, you are trying to build up capital but have a very cautious nature, look at the low-risk growth group. Most of the investments here do not involve any exposure to equities. And those that do are designed to smooth out the effects of any sharp setbacks. Of course, you cannot expect to get such high returns from these investments as from those in the high-growth category. But never assume that high returns are guaranteed if you take high risks.

The income categories also allow you to find investments which suit your specific requirements. Note that only one category offers guarantees on both income and capital – and that of course is only the capital without inflation proofing. That is the most cautious collection. Some of the investments we have put in the 'no guarantees' and 'income guaranteed' categories are pretty hairy. (see Top Tip on page 15).

● **Some caveats.** Categorizing investments like this is a contentious, some would say foolhardy, endeavour. And any reader who follows our categories blindly could do themselves financial damage. We have tried the categories out on some financial advisers, and met several disagreements on precisely which category particular investments should be in.

But there are also two more serious problems.

First, the same investment can produce very different results, depending on how you use it, how long you hold it for and when you buy and sell it. Hold a gilt to maturity and you have no market risk; trade it and you do.

Second, few investments are generic products. Which shares you choose will have a big effect on how well or badly you do. Any unit trust performance table will show big variations between the results from different funds in the same sector. And, at the top of the risk scale, some biotech companies or enterprise investment schemes may make your fortune; others will be buried without trace.

The fact that we have included two investments in the same box does not mean they are of equal merit.

And then of course there is tax. The same gilt will produce different returns to people liable to different rates of tax.

HOW THE FT CAN HELP

Gilts prices

Even safe investments, such as gilt-edged securities, have pitfalls for the unwary. Our regular **gilts prices table** helps you avoid them. It appears in the second section of the newspaper Tuesday to Friday and in the first on Saturday.

Many income seekers buy gilts because they have a government guarantee behind them. Our table shows what's on offer. Gilts represent government borrowings and are traded on the stock market, until the government repays its debt. Most gilts have a preset repayment date, known as the 'redemption date'. The *FT* table lists the stocks in order of repayment, with 'shorts' (stocks due to be repaid within five years) first, then 'mediums' (5–15 years) and 'longs' (over 15 years). Then come undated stocks (which have no fixed repayment date) and index-linked stocks, where both capital and interest payments are linked to inflation.

Our illustration here shows the beginning of the 'mediums'. The name of the stock shows what the nominal interest rate is and when it will be repaid. Thus Conversion 9½ per cent 2004 pays interest at the rate of £9.50 each year on every £100 of stock, and will be repaid on 25 October 2004. But that does not mean you get 9½ per cent whenever you put £100 into this stock. When interest rates are substantially higher than 9½ per cent, the market price of £100 nominal of stock is likely to drop well below £100 ('below par'), to bring the yield up to market levels. When interest rates are lower, the market price will rise above £100 ('above par'). So new buyers get whatever the going rate is. Thus, in this example, taken when interest rates were well below 9½ per cent, the price is over £121 per £100 of stock, and the annual interest rate a new purchaser would get is 7.8 per cent (shown as 'interest yield' in the table).

UK GILTS PRICES

Notes	Yield int	Yield Red	Price £	+ or -	52 week High	52 week Low	Undated
Five to Fifteen Years							Consols 4pc
Treas 6 ½pc 2003	6.17	5.32	105½	-½	105 1/16	100½	War Loan 3½
Treas 11½pc 2001-4	10.20	5.93	112 13/16 xd	-1/16	114 7/8	110 11/16	Conv 3½pc
Treas 10pc 2004 .... ☆	8.21	5.46	121¾	...	121 13/16	115 13/16	Treas 3pc '6
Funding 3½pc 1999-4.....	3.64	4.25	96 1/8	+1/16	96 1/8	87 13/16	Consols 2½
Conv 9½pc 2004	7.84	5.37	121½	-½	121¼	114 1/16	Treas. 2½pc

● 'Tap' stock. All UK Gilts are tax-free to non-residents on application. E Auction basis calculated by HSBC Greenwell from Bank of England closing prices. ☆ Indicative price.

But that's a bit of an illusion. For between now and October 2004 you are set to lose over £21 of your original capital investment, because you will only get £100 when the stock is repaid. The second yield in the table, the 'redemption yield' takes account of any capital loss or gain. That is why it is more than two percentage points lower than the interest yield. Redemption yields are what professional investors look at.

The second stock in the table looks particularly tempting. Treasury 11½ pc 2001–4 has an interest yield of over 10 per cent, a final expiry date of 2004, and looks a bargain at under £113 per 100. Alas, no. When a stock has a choice of redemption dates, and is standing above par, the Treasury will normally repay it as early as possible – 19 March 2001 in this case. The market is pricing it on this assumption. So, although it is officially a medium-dated stock, it is really a short in disguise.

Note also the 'ex-d' next to the share price. Seven working days before a stock pays its dividend it goes ex-dividend, meaning that the buyer cannot claim the dividend from the seller. Our snapshot was taken on 17 September 1998, and the stock was scheduled to pay its dividend on 19 September. A useful warning.

And all those horrible fractions in the prices? Don't worry. They went at the end of October 1998, when the gilt market went decimal.

TOP TIP

High-income bonds
Guaranteed high-income bonds sound too good to be true, and they are. Avoid them.

The bonds, issued by life assurance companies, promise an unusually high fixed income for the life of the contract, usually around five years. The snag is that if stockmarkets move against you, you may not get all of your capital back. Indeed, in some instances, the total return (income plus return of capital) can be less than the initial investment.

These bonds have been extensively sold to retired people who rely on the income for their everyday expenses. But they cannot afford to risk their capital and often do not realize that they are doing so.

An additional problem is that the name is confusingly similar to that of the conventional guaranteed-income bonds, also sold by insurance companies: these guarantee both a fixed income and return of the original capital at the end of the contract term.

The precise terms of guaranteed high-income bonds vary. Most of the early ones linked the proportion of capital returned to the performance of a single stock market index, often the FTSE 100. Subsequent ones have often had links to a couple of different world stock market indices, and the nature of the links also varies considerably.

In 1998 the Treasury banned future sales of certain types of high-income bond. In previous years, selling methods had been criticized by the Personal Investment Authority Ombudsman after several thousands of complaints from the public. And the actuaries' associations had criticized sales literature.

High yield has always been a sign of high risk in equity and bond markets. Other products designed to produce an unusually high income may also eat into your capital. Voluntary annuities provide a guaranteed income for life, but none of the capital is repaid. And some split capital investment trusts have 'annuity' income shares, which offer a high, though variable, income during their life, but only a token repayment of capital when the trust is wound up.

Choosing a broker or financial adviser
Finding the right person to help you with your investment strategy is as important as the strategy itself

The cynic's definition of a stockbroker as 'someone who invests all your money until there is none of it left' is of course unfair. But there is no doubt that finding a good investment adviser can be a fraught business.

The very term 'financial adviser' has acquired mixed connotations for investors in recent years – the £11bn pensions mis-selling scandal showed that some independent financial advisers (IFAs) were no more immune than life assurance salesmen to giving poor quality, commission-driven advice.

But there are also excellent advisers, who will provide a top-quality service for a reasonable fee. The trick is to sort out the wheat from the chaff. This is easier said than done, given that there are literally thousands of authorized firms of advisers competing for your business. But it is worth taking some time and effort to find a good one – it could make a huge difference to your future financial health.

● **The services available.** First you need to be clear what you want advice on and what you want your adviser to do for you. Financial planning and investment advice and management are different skills.

Financial planning provides a long-term strategy to help you reach your objectives. It provides answers to questions like: 'How can I make sure I have enough money to live on when I retire or to put the children through private schools?' These answers will probably include recommendations to invest so much a year in a pension scheme and so much in individual savings accounts. And they may well build in estimates of the capital growth and income expected from these schemes.

Investment is concerned with picking and monitoring assets designed to achieve such targets without unacceptable risk. It involves either selecting portfolios (collections) of shares, fixed-interest stocks, cash and other assets to do the job, or using packaged investments, such as unit and investment trusts or life and pension policies.

Some people like taking their own investment decisions. If you do not want any help, go to an execution-only stockbroker. If you want some advice but want to run your own affairs, you need investment advice. But if you want to leave all the day-to-day decisions to someone else, you need investment management.

● **Who does what?** The boundaries between different types of company have become blurred in recent years – some accountants and solicitors now have fully integrated IFA arms, for example, while a number of fund managers and private-client banks offer portfolio-management services similar to those offered by stockbrokers. The chart on page 20 provides a broad guide to the main types of investment advice services.

● **Finding the right service.** Your options will depend on how much money you have. The £100,000 cut-off point quoted in the chart is very much a rule-of-thumb guide. A few investment advisers or managers have a minimum investment level of less than £100,000, while some have a much higher threshold. Mercury Asset Management, for example, requires you to invest at least £250,000 before it will run a portfolio of managed funds and at least £1m to run a portfolio containing shares as well as funds.

One good reason for this apparent arrogance is costs. For example, a balanced equity portfolio needs a minimum number of stocks in it to spread the risks. If the total amount of money available means that the value of each holding is relatively low, costs will be relatively high if you go to an investment manager. That makes the portfolio uneconomic unless you run it yourself.

If you have much less than £100,000 but want a portfolio managed on your behalf, one alternative is to go for a managed-funds service where the adviser runs a portfolio of unit trusts and other funds on your behalf. Performance varies. But, if you go this route, remember that the charge for the adviser's service comes on top of the charges on the underlying investments. Few funds consistently produce a good enough performance to counteract the effect of doubled charges.

The £100,000 cut-off point also serves as a rough guide in the area of general financial advice. The level of fees charged by most specialized financial planners will usually mean it is not worth paying for the very comprehensive advice service unless you have at least £100,000 to invest or need advice on a specialized area, such as financial planning for a business partnership. But there are exceptions to this rule.

All IFAs will offer general investment advice, and many set no minimum on the amount you have to invest. But the quality of this advice is likely to be variable. Many IFAs do not have specialized knowledge of shares and investment trusts or even, in some cases, unit trusts. If you opt for an IFA paid mainly by commission, rather than fees, you also run the risk that the advice you get will be biased towards packaged products, such as life assurance bonds or unit trust personal equity plans that pay high levels of commission.

Once you have decided the type of service you are interested in, contact the relevant professional bodies – most now offer directories that give helpful information on what each member firm offers.

• **Grilling the experts.** The next step is to arrange interviews with the firms that you are interested in. Draw up a short list of points you want to cover with the adviser. These could include:

• **The level of service offered.** Who will be in charge of your portfolio or giving you investment advice? What information will they give you and what extra services such as capital gains tax statements are included? What research resources does the firm have to back up its advice and recommendations?

• **Investment performance.** What evidence does the firm have of its investment record? Does it use the standard portfolio benchmarks (see pages 22–4) or does it have internal performance guidelines?

• **Qualifications and experience.** Ask what professional qualifications and relevant experience the adviser or investment manager you will be dealing with has.

All advisers must get a basic qualification before they can give

WHICH IS THE RIGHT ADVISER FOR YOU?

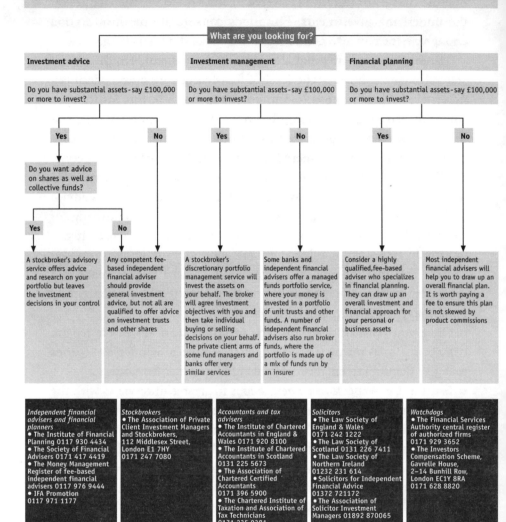

What are you looking for?

Investment advice

Do you have substantial assets - say £100,000 or more to invest?

Yes

Do you want advice on shares as well as collective funds?

Yes

A stockbroker's advisory service offers advice and research on your portfolio but leaves the investment decisions in your control

No

Any competent fee-based independent financial adviser should provide general investment advice, but not all are qualified to offer advice on investment trusts and other shares

No

Investment management

Do you have substantial assets - say £100,000 or more to invest?

Yes

A stockbroker's discretionary portfolio management service will invest the assets on your behalf. The broker will agree investment objectives with you and then take individual buying or selling decisions on your behalf. The private client arms of some fund managers and banks offer very similar services

No

Some banks and independent financial advisers offer a managed funds portfolio service, where your money is invested in a portfolio of unit trusts and other funds. A number of independent financial advisers also run broker funds, where the portfolio is made up of a mix of funds run by an insurer

Financial planning

Do you have substantial assets - say £100,000 or more to invest?

Yes

Consider a highly qualified, fee-based adviser who specializes in financial planning. They can draw up an overall investment and financial approach for your personal or business assets

No

Most independent financial advisers will help you to draw up an overall financial plan. It is worth paying a fee to ensure this plan is not skewed by product commissions

---

Independent financial advisers and financial planners
• The Institute of Financial Planning 0117 930 4434
• The Society of Financial Advisers 0171 417 4419
• The Money Management Register of fee-based independent financial advisers 0117 976 9444
• IFA Promotion 0117 971 1177

Stockbrokers
• The Association of Private Client Investment Managers and Stockbrokers, 112 Middlesex Street, London E1 7HY 0171 247 7080

Accountants and tax advisers
• The Institute of Chartered Accountants in England & Wales 0171 920 8100
• The Institute of Chartered Accountants in Scotland 0131 225 5673
• The Association of Chartered Certified Accountants 0171 396 5900
• The Chartered Institute of Taxation and Association of Tax Technicians 0171 235 9381

Solicitors
• The Law Society of England & Wales 0171 242 1222
• The Law Society of Scotland 0131 226 7411
• The Law Society of Northern Ireland 01232 231 614
• Solicitors for Independent Financial Advice 01372 721172
• The Association of Solicitor Investment Managers 01892 870065

Watchdogs
• The Financial Services Authority central register of authorized firms 0171 929 3652
• The Investors Compensation Scheme, Gavrelle House, 2–14 Bunhill Row, London EC1Y 8RA 0171 628 8820

unsupervised advice to the public – the main ones are the Investment Advice Certificate (IAC) and the Financial Planning Certificate (FPC). Most stockbrokers will take the Registered Persons exam instead, as this allows them to give advice on equities.

Advisers can take tougher exams should they want to. The main one for general financial advice is the Advanced Financial Planning Certificate (AFPC). At a higher level still, there is the Institute of Financial Planning's fellowship exams and, on the equities side, the Securities Institute's diploma qualifications.

● **The costs.** What are the charges, including dealing commissions, likely to be? For financial advice, is the adviser fee-based or paid by commission from product sales?

INVESTORS COMPENSATION SCHEME

A financial safety net

The Investors Compensation Scheme (ICS) had its tenth birthday in August 1998. Over 11,500 investors had cause to join in the celebrations – they are the recipients of the £130m the ICS has paid since its inception to clients of investment and financial advice firms that have gone bust.

The scheme clearly provides a very useful safety net. But safety-conscious investors should also be aware of its limitations. It covers only firms that are authorized under the Financial Services Act – if you are in any doubt whether a firm or adviser falls into this category, check the register run by the Financial Services Authority. The ICS also has a £48,000 ceiling on the amount it will pay out to any investor – 100 per cent of the first £30,000 of your losses and 90 per cent of the next £20,000.

In fairness to stockbrokers and investment managers, it should be said that they account for proportionately very few of the 380 failed firms that the ICS has dealt with, most of which were independent financial advisers.

None the less, if you are planning to invest a lot more than £48,000 with a firm and it does not have a giant parent company (such as a clearing bank), it is worth asking what, if any, safety arrangements it has made. Some brokers, for example, have bought insurance cover to give investors additional protection should the firm become insolvent.

To claim from the scheme. You can only claim from the ICS if the investment firm involved has stopped trading. Write to the scheme giving brief details of your claim, including the full name and address of the firm, how much money you invested with the firm, what the type of investment was and why you believe you have got a claim.

Charges

Comparing the costs of using different advisers can be difficult because charging structures vary widely. As a rule-of-thumb guide:

● Stockbrokers charge a mix of dealing commission (usually a percentage of the value of the deal, subject to a minimum charge) and regular fees.

● Independent advisers are generally paid from product sales, although some offer investors the option of paying fees (changed on an hourly basis). A few are entirely fee-based, as are accountants and solicitors. Check the details of the charges. If the adviser is fee-based, for example, will all sales commissions be rebated to you, even if they exceed the amount of the fees?

HOW THE FT CAN HELP

Private investor indices

How can you gauge how well your stockbroker or investment manager is running your portfolio? The honest answer is 'not easily'. But there are tools that can help you.

These include the **private investor indices** which the *FT* publishes in Weekend Money every Saturday. These indices, produced jointly by FTSE International and APCIMS, the stockbrokers' trade body, are designed to act as a benchmark against which you can monitor the performance of your own portfolio.

The indices show the investment performance in terms of capital (excluding income, in other words) of three model portfolios: an income one, which contains mainly UK shares and bonds; a growth one, which is much more heavily weighted towards shares; and a balanced one, which is a mix of UK and overseas shares, bonds and cash.

These weightings are based on portfolios run by twenty-four firms of stockbrokers. The models may be adjusted from time to time to reflect changes in these 'real life' portfolios. The exact make-up of each model portfolio is given in the footnote to the table each week.

The table also shows the performance over the same time periods, ranging from one month to five years, of the three indices which are used to calculate the performance of the portfolios themselves. These are the FTSE All-Share index, which reflects the overall performance of the UK stock market; the FT/S&P-AWI (Ex UK) index which reflects the performance of world stock markets other than the UK; and the FTSE UK Gilts (All Stocks) index.

■ Private Investor Indices

Capital performance		% change			
	10/9/1998	1 month	3 months	One year	Five years
Growth	2500.63	−8.41	−13.65	0.69	46.47
Balanced	2291.02	−6.40	−10.96	2.78	40.34
Income	1938.27	−3.72	−7.40	5.62	29.69
FTSE All-Share index	2395.67	−8.74	−15.88	3.44	58.51
FT/S&P-AWI (Ex UK)	217.10	−11.39	−14.47	−7.40	36.36
FTSE UK Gilts (All Stocks)	161.27	2.83	3.65	8.94	6.16
RPI	163.00	−0.24	1.37	2.84	14.87

Calculated by FTSE Intl. in association with APCIMS. © FTSE International Ltd 1998. All rights reserved.

The private investor indices are meant to be indicative, rather than precise. They are not meant to be an absolute measure to which brokers aspire. For one thing, the indices take no account of the effects of charges and tax. What is more, they will not reflect exactly the asset mix of your individual portfolio, which can have a dramatic effect on performance. If, to take an extreme example, you had agreed with your broker to invest most of your portfolio in emerging markets and (as happened in 1998) those markets collapsed, it would clearly be unreasonable to blame the broker for doing much worse than the growth private investor index.

Brokers are all too aware of the dangers that private investors will use the benchmarks as a stick to beat them with for perceived poor performance. Some refuse to use either the FTSE/APCIMS indices or the similar indices which are published by the WM Company. They argue that the whole point of getting a broker to manage a portfolio for you, rather than simply buying a unit trust or other managed fund, is the bespoke service – you can dictate exactly what investment objectives you have and influence both the asset mix and the stock selection.

This argument has some validity. But, provided investors use the indices sensibly, they can be a useful yardstick. Of course, the benchmark information needs interpreting carefully. If, however, your portfolio has performed substantially worse than the comparable private investor index, it is at least worth asking your stockbroker why.

TOP TIP

Safeguarding perks

If you own shares that offer valuable perks, such as the cheap ferry crossings offered on some P&O stock, be careful before you put them into a stockbroker's nominee account.

With these accounts, shares are held by the broker (the legal owner) on behalf of the shareholder (the beneficial owner). Most companies – P&O is an exception, as are Gieves Group and Barratt Developments – will now extend their perks to shareholders in a nominee account. But the onus falls on the shareholder or their stockbroker to claim any perks, rather than the company to deliver them. Companies cannot contact shareholders directly because, under the nominee system, the names of individuals do not appear on the share register.

Usually, you have to ask the broker to write to the company

concerned confirming you are a shareholder and that you own enough shares to qualify. Some stockbrokers will attempt to collect perks for nominee holders as a matter of course.

One way round this problem is if you are an active investor member of Crest, the paperless settlement system. This avoids any problems with perks because your name appears on the share register. But it will not work for the main P&O stock that offers perks – the 5.5 per cent redeemable non-cumulative preferred stock (also known as concessionary stock) – since this is one of the stocks which has opted not to be in Crest. It is also not worth opting for sponsored membership, which can cost £100 or more a year, simply because of share perks.

If you own shares with good perks and your broker does not offer to collect those perks as part of its nominee service, the simplest solution is to hold the stock separately yourself, outside the nominee account.

Bear in mind, however, that there are few cases where the shareholder perks are so valuable that they alone justify buying the shares.

Route through the investment universe

*The basic building blocks of all investment portfolios are cash,
fixed-interest securities and equities. Their typical returns vary, and
so do their characteristics. In theory, the higher the risk, the higher
the return*

This has not always proved true in practice, but it is sufficiently true for there to be considerable agreement on what kind of investor should hold them in what circumstances. Since they tend to respond differently at different stages of the economic cycle, there are also good and bad times to buy and sell them.

The trouble is that the factors that affect long-term returns on securities are often not the same as those which trigger short-term price movements. And it is possible to lose a lot of money by being over logical.

Interest rates are probably the most important single short-term influence. When rates are high and rising, deposit accounts suck money out of shares and fixed-interest stocks, partly because returns on cash have become more competitive, and partly because high interest rates are generally bad news for companies and so for share prices. When rates are low and falling, the tide flows the other way.

● **Cash.** Depositing your money with a bank or building society, or in a unit trust paying money-market interest rates, is the safest option. And the return available on cash is used as a benchmark for riskier types of investment. It only makes sense to buy fixed-interest stocks or shares if you expect them to produce higher returns than you can get on cash.

● **Fixed interest.** There are two main types of fixed-interest stocks. Gilts represent government debts and are traded on the stock market.

Corporate bonds work in much the same way, but do not have the government's rock solid guarantee behind them. And the additional risk means that investors demand higher returns from corporate bonds than from gilts.

There are two ways of investing in gilts and other fixed-interest stocks. Safety-first investors can use them to lock in a given rate of interest for a longer period than is normally possible with a deposit by buying and holding until the preset redemption date. Doing this protects them from market risk. The much riskier alternative is to trade bonds actively, aiming to buy before prices rise and sell before they fall.

Like cash, conventional gilts are vulnerable to inflation. But nowadays investors have an alternative that removes the need to worry about inflation: index-linked gilts.

Foreign currency bonds are another possibility, but they involve an additional exchange rate risk.

● **U K equities.** Shares are riskier than cash or gilts. But since the 1960s they have become the staple of life and pension funds, because they offer the prospect of long-term capital and income growth. Over periods of a decade or more, share prices track company profitability very closely. And the basic trend in profits has been upwards, as the economy itself has grown, albeit with wobbles when the economic cycle turns down. Equities are also seen as relatively inflation-proof, unlike cash and gilts, although they often suffer a profits hiccup when inflation starts rising.

There are two snags. First, in the short term, the market as a whole often diverges substantially from its underlying trend. Second, prices of individual companies often diverge substantially from the index.

So, if you buy at a bad time, you can well lose money by investing in the stock market, even if you buy a fund designed to track the whole market. And if you invest in individual shares, you can lose money, even when the market is rising.

There are two ways to make money from equities. Either invest for the very long term, and forget about it. Or outsmart the market. Later articles in this Guide explain some popular techniques for doing the latter.

BLUFFER'S GUIDE TO THE INVESTMENT UNIVERSE

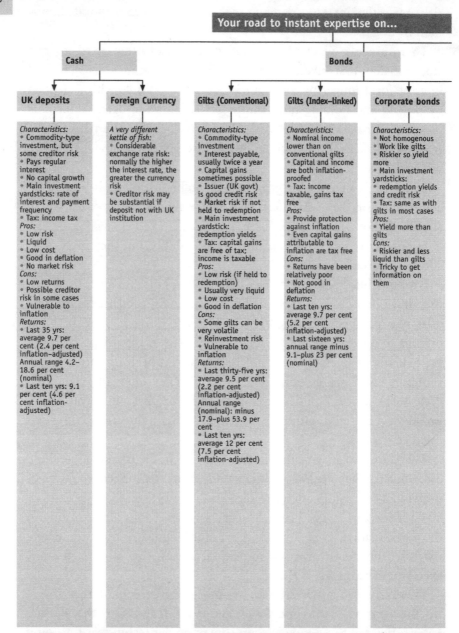

Your road to instant expertise on...

Cash

Bonds

UK deposits

Characteristics:
* Commodity-type investment, but some creditor risk
* Pays regular interest
* No capital growth
* Main investment yardsticks: rate of interest and payment frequency
* Tax: income tax
Pros:
* Low risk
* Liquid
* Low cost
* Good in deflation
* No market risk
Cons:
* Low returns
* Possible creditor risk in some cases
* Vulnerable to inflation
Returns:
* Last 35 yrs: average 9.7 per cent (2.4 per cent inflation–adjusted) Annual range 4.2–18.6 per cent (nominal)
* Last ten yrs: 9.1 per cent (4.6 per cent inflation-adjusted)

Foreign Currency

A very different kettle of fish:
* Considerable exchange rate risk: normally the higher the interest rate, the greater the currency risk
* Creditor risk may be substantial if deposit not with UK institution

Gilts (Conventional)

Characteristics:
* Commodity-type investment
* Interest payable, usually twice a year
* Capital gains sometimes possible
* Issuer (UK govt) is good credit risk
* Market risk if not held to redemption
* Main investment yardstick: redemption yields
* Tax: capital gains are free of tax; income is taxable
Pros:
* Low risk (if held to redemption)
* Usually very liquid
* Low cost
* Good in deflation
Cons:
* Some gilts can be very volatile
* Reinvestment risk
* Vulnerable to inflation
Returns:
* Last thirty-five yrs: average 9.5 per cent (2.2 per cent inflation-adjusted) Annual range (nominal): minus 17.9–plus 53.9 per cent
* Last ten yrs: average 12 per cent (7.5 per cent inflation-adjusted)

Gilts (Index–linked)

Characteristics:
* Nominal income lower than on conventional gilts
* Capital and income are both inflation-proofed
* Tax: income taxable, gains tax free
Pros:
* Provide protection against inflation
* Even capital gains attributable to inflation are tax free
Cons:
* Returns have been relatively poor
* Not good in deflation
Returns:
* Last ten yrs: average 9.7 per cent (5.2 per cent inflation-adjusted)
* Last sixteen yrs: annual range minus 9.1–plus 23 per cent (nominal)

Corporate bonds

Characteristics:
* Not homogenous
* Work like gilts
* Riskier so yield more
* Main investment yardsticks:
 * redemption yields and credit risk
* Tax: same as with gilts in most cases
Pros:
* Yield more than gilts
Cons:
* Riskier and less liquid than gilts
* Tricky to get information on them

Statistics
The figures for gross (pre-tax) annual total returns are taken from PDFM's pension fund indicators. Returns to private investors will in most cases be substantially lower. The domestic house price figures, showing changes in capital values, come from Nationwide.

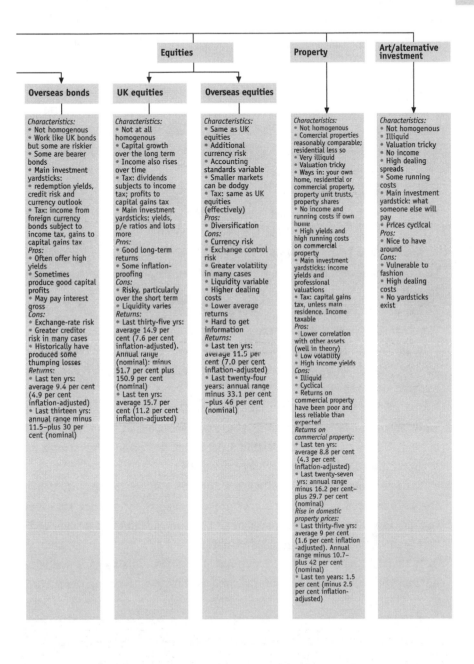

Equities			Property	Art/alternative investment

Overseas bonds	UK equities	Overseas equities		

Overseas bonds

Characteristics:
• Not homogenous
• Work like UK bonds but some are riskier
• Some are bearer bonds
• Main investment yardsticks:
• redemption yields, credit risk and currency outlook
• Tax: income from foreign currency bonds subject to income tax, gains to capital gains tax
Pros:
• Often offer high yields
• Sometimes produce good capital profits
• May pay interest gross
Cons:
• Exchange-rate risk
• Greater creditor risk in many cases
• Historically have produced some thumping losses
Returns:
• Last ten yrs: average 9.4 per cent (4.9 per cent inflation-adjusted)
• Last thirteen yrs: annual range minus 11.5–plus 30 per cent (nominal)

UK equities

Characteristics:
• Not at all homogenous
• Capital growth over the long term
• Income also rises over time
• Tax: dividends subjects to income tax; profits to capital gains tax
• Main investment yardsticks: yields, p/e ratios and lots more
Pros:
• Good long-term returns
• Some inflation-proofing
Cons:
• Risky, particularly over the short term
• Liquidity varies
Returns:
• Last thirty-five yrs: average 14.9 per cent (7.6 per cent inflation-adjusted). Annual range (nominal): minus 51.7 per cent plus 150.9 per cent (nominal)
• Last ten yrs: average 15.7 per cent (11.2 per cent inflation-adjusted)

Overseas equities

Characteristics:
• Same as UK equities
• Additional currency risk
• Accounting standards variable
• Smaller markets can be dodgy
• Tax: same as UK equities (effectively)
Pros:
• Diversification
Cons:
• Currency risk
• Exchange control risk
• Greater volatility in many cases
• Liquidity variable
• Higher dealing costs
• Lower average returns
• Hard to get information
Returns:
• Last ten yrs: average 11.5 per cent (7.0 per cent inflation-adjusted)
• Last twenty-four years: annual range minus 33.1 per cent –plus 46 per cent (nominal)

Property

Characteristics:
• Not homogenous
• Comercial properties reasonably comparable; residential less so
• Very illiquid
• Valuation tricky
• Ways in: your own home, residential or commercial property, property unit trusts, property shares
• No income and running costs if own home
• High yields and high running costs on commercial property
• Main investment yardsticks: income yields and professional valuations
• Tax: capital gains tax, unless main residence. Income taxable
Pros:
• Lower correlation with other assets (well in theory)
• Low volatility
• High income yields
Cons:
• Illiquid
• Cyclical
• Returns on commercial property have been poor and less reliable than expected
Returns on commercial property:
• Last ten yrs: average 8.8 per cent (4.3 per cent inflation-adjusted)
• Last twenty-seven yrs: annual range minus 16.2 per cent– plus 29.7 per cent (nominal)
Rise in domestic property prices:
• Last thirty-five yrs: average 9 per cent (1.6 per cent inflation-adjusted). Annual range minus 10.7– plus 42 per cent (nominal)
• Last ten years: 1.5 per cent (minus 2.5 per cent inflation-adjusted)

Art/alternative investment

Characteristics:
• Not homogenous
• Illiquid
• Valuation tricky
• No income
• High dealing spreads
• Some running costs
• Main investment yardstick: what someone else will pay
• Prices cyclical
Pros:
• Nice to have around
Cons:
• Vulnerable to fashion
• High dealing costs
• No yardsticks exist

● **Overseas equities.** The arguments are the same as those for UK shares, but there is an additional currency risk for sterling investors.

● **Property.** Many individual investors already have a large proportion of their total assets in property in the shape of their home. Commercial property used to be popular with professional investors because it was seen as an inflation hedge, but index-linked gilts now fulfil this function better.

CAUTIONARY TALES

Gilt-edged con trick

Name a security which has lost investors 97.7 per cent of their money over the last sixty-seven years, if you adjust for inflation.

Answer: War Loan; a so-called gilt-edged stock. And that is despite the fact that the recent fall in gilt yields has driven its price higher than it has been for years.

The British government may never have actually defaulted, but the 1932 War Loan conversion was a massive swindle. And the loser was the patriotic/gullible British investing public. The story provides a vivid example of how vulnerable conventional gilts are to inflation, and how dangerous undated stocks can be.

The original 5 per cent War Loan issue, made in 1917 to finance the First World War and due to be repaid in 1947, was enormous at £2bn. By 1932 it accounted for a quarter of the National Debt. And just paying the interest on it sopped up two-fifths of all income tax receipts.

The government could afford neither to service it nor to repay it. Hence the brilliant idea of persuading investors to swap it for a stock that was cheaper to service and would never need to be repaid: the new 3½ per cent War Loan which had no set repayment date.

It sounds a hard sell. But by rigging the market, organizing a publicity blitz and bribing the brokers with fat commissions, the government managed it.

Today the once mighty War Loan issue accounts for less than 1 per cent of the gilts market. But even if some future government were to repay it, there would be no real reparation to the generation of investors whose savings were swallowed by inflation.

Moral: *caveat emptor*, even when it is the government doing the selling.

HOW THE FT CAN HELP

London share service

The *Financial Times* **London share service** is an institution. It not only tells you the previous day's closing price for the majority of quoted UK companies' shares, but it also gives you some rough and ready tools with which to weigh up each company. The service appears at the back of the second section on Monday to Friday, and in the first section on Saturday.

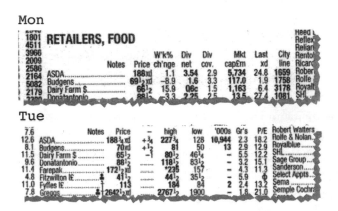

The companies are grouped in business sectors designed for professional investors. For analysts tend to assess a share by comparing its vital statistics with those of its peer group. Thus a food retailer, such as Asda, is compared with other food retailers, such as J. Sainsbury and Tesco, not with food producers, such as Express Dairies.

This is partly because they are genuinely more comparable, but also because many investors have standard 'weightings' in each sector. If, say, food retailers account for 3 per cent of the All-Share index a fund manager might keep roughly 3 per cent of his portfolio in food retailers, but have a disproportionate chunk of that 3 per cent in Asda because he prefers it to Tesco.

The share service on Mondays provides background information, since there will have been no stock market changes since Friday. Arguably the most useful figure is the market capitalization, which gives you a quick fix on the size of the company. Professional investors are mainly interested in large companies. So do not be surprised if a small company looks out of line with larger rivals.

The percentage change over the week shows where the action has been. In our example, Budgens was out of favour because investors were worried by its talks with Booker. Then comes the dividend information: how much was it and how safe is it? The higher the cover, the safer. Budgen's cover of over 3 is comfortable. (A flip across to Booker on the other page showed an uncovered dividend.)

The last xd date is a bit more esoteric. Share prices allow for future dividend payments. But soon after the payment has been announced, they go ex-dividend, meaning that the person who buys the share thereafter cannot claim the dividend from the share's former owner. The price falls to reflect this. And until the dividend is actually paid out the price will be quoted xd – as Budgens is here.

But the main investment statistics are in the Tuesday to Saturday service. The dividend yield and price/earnings ratio may be considered a bit primitive nowadays, but they are still popular yardsticks. And any major anomalies are worth investigating. The high and low give you a rough idea of whether the shares are on a winning or a losing streak. And again, if one share is falling while the rest of the sector is rising, it is worth finding out why.

Volume figures show where the smart money is going – or leaving – but they need to be taken in context. Large companies are traded much more heavily than small ones. And it is normal for volumes to be high when a company makes an announcement. But if you are following a company's price every day, you should notice whether the volume is unusually heavy for no obvious reason.

Share price spreads

Do not ask the price, ask the spread. That is the advice from retail stockbrokers. Wide spreads between buying and selling prices used to be a problem peculiar to the shares of small companies. Nowadays it has infected shares of the largest companies too, at least early in the morning.

The prices in the *Financial Times'* London share service are 'mid prices', half way between the buying and selling prices. But the width of the spread between the two varies, with those on illiquid shares – ones that change hands infrequently – much higher than those on frequently traded shares in the FTSE 100. The wider the spread, the further the price has to rise before an investor is showing a profit on his holding.

Some of the widest spreads occur on unquoted shares. A spot check on Arsenal football club, for example, showed a price of £3,600 if you were buying, £3,000 if you were selling. On the exchange itself, the traditional rule of thumb is that the touch (the difference between the best buying and selling price available anywhere) on a blue chip should be around 0.5 per cent, but it can go up to 15 per cent or more on a rarely traded share in a small company.

It is not surprising that small companies can be illiquid. What does shock many private investors is that spreads in major Footsie

34

companies can rise to 6 or 7 per cent early in the day. These rogue spreads are the side-effect of the stock exchange's adoption of electronic trading for Footsie companies.

Retail stockbrokers suggest some ways investors can protect themselves:

● Beware of dealing by post. You may save on the broking commission but lose on the price.

● Do not deal early or late in the day.

● If you cannot avoid it, leave the order with your broker, and place a 'limit' on it, which gives your broker a price target.

● When your broker quotes you a spread, ask whether that is a normal spread for this share. If it is abnormally wide, the best advice is to wait and deal later.

Keeping a level head

We instinctively understand that big rewards, like those that come from a 20–1 horse race winner, involve a high risk of losing our money too. But the precise nature of the relationship between risk and return requires careful study

Ordinary people have a notoriously distorted understanding of risk. A typical example is the person who gets worried sick about going on an aircraft to Spain, but not when it comes to a family car trip on a Sunday afternoon, although statistically speaking the risks are much higher for the car journey.

It is much the same with savings and investments. Amateur punters will often commit their money to very dubious deposit institutions for the sake of a percentage point or two of extra return. They will chase fashionable stock market investments like biotechnology shares (well, they *were* fashionable a few years ago) without being fully aware that big upside gains in the past may be systematically linked to big downside risks in the future.

Professional investors have a more rigorous approach to risk, even though the most sophisticated practitioners got it badly wrong at the troubled hedge fund Long-Term Capital Management. 'Risk control' teams have been established by all the big investment management groups. Their activities involve complex mathematics and extensive historical databases. However, the analysis has to begin with some basics.

Classic US investment theory, in fact, has started off by defining zero-risk investment in terms of treasury bills – short-term government paper that normally has an average life of a few weeks or months. Because repayment is guaranteed by the government, there is no credit risk (at least, there is not in a stable country; we shall leave Russia, which defaulted on its treasury bills in August 1998, out of this). And because the term of the bills to maturity is so short, the capital value will scarcely change when interest rates rise or fall. Private investors, alternatively, could consider a short-term deposit with a prime banking institution to be a riskless asset.

This takes for granted that investment risk can be defined as the volatility of capital values (or more strictly, in terms of capital market theory, as the volatility of investment returns) over specified short periods in absolute terms. In fact, from the point of view of diversified personal investors, this is a useful approach, because it helps comparisons across a range of savings media such as building society deposits and various bond and equity unit trusts as well as individual shares.

There is nevertheless quite a lot of controversy among professional investors about the nature of risk. Many prefer to talk in terms of their risks against their benchmarks. Some benchmarks are expressed in terms of an index or a combination of indices. Others are peer-group benchmarks – related to the performance of comparable funds.

Unit trust managers, for instance, are primarily worried about their performance against the average fund in their sectors because that (more than anything else) determines whether net sales will be good or bad.

The vogue for benchmarking has spread to private client managers, and FTSE International, the *FT*'s associate company, publishes three private investor indices in association with APCIMS, the private client stockbroker trade association (see pages 22–3).

A portfolio that closely matches the structure of, for instance, the Private Investor Growth Index will have shown little movement against it in recent months. On one definition, its risk can, therefore, be said to be low. On the other hand, in absolute terms, its value is likely to have fallen by 16 per cent in the past three months or so. The client may feel that the risks are quite high. Both concepts are valid, but they need to be properly understood. Risk (or volatility of returns) relative to a benchmark is often measured as a tracking error. This uses the concept of standard deviation, a mathematical tool that defines the distribution of observations around a mean, where these follow a normal bell-shaped probability curve.

Tracking error is in some respects an unfortunate term, and alternatives such as active risk may be preferable. A portfolio that has a zero tracking error against the FTSE All-Share Index is, in effect, a tracker fund. This is fine as long as your fund manager admits the fact and charges you the low fees appropriate for tracker funds.

If the manager is to have a realistic hope of beating the index, however, he must manage the portfolio to show a significant tracking error (or active risk). The greater his ambitions to outperform, the greater that tracking error must be.

Risky assets must hold out the hope of higher returns (always defined as total returns, combining income with capital gains or losses). Otherwise investors, who are naturally risk-averse, and would take something for nothing if they could get it, would not hold volatile investments.

Usually the historically recorded market returns make sense in this context. In the short run, the markets can be erratic, but over the period 1986–97 the average annual gross return on short-term sterling deposits was 9.1 per cent and the equivalent return on the safest gilts, index-linked, was 9.7 per cent. Fixed-interest gilts, which tend to show a greater volatility of returns than the linkers, returned 12 per cent and UK equities 15.7 per cent. It does not always work out so neatly, however, even over quite long periods.

For several decades after the war, gilts returned much less in total return terms than risk-free bank deposits. This was because rising inflation was reflected in money-market interest rates, but had not been anticipated by buyers of long-term bonds, which persistently fell in price so that total returns were poor.

In the equity market, risk can be measured in two ways. There is an overall market risk because the indices can go up and down by substantial margins – as we have seen in 1997–8. But individual company stocks can have their own specific risks, relating to their particular circumstances.

Specific risk can be diversified away, and therefore does not carry a statistical probability of being associated with an extra return. Investors who accept high stock risks in their portfolios will only be rewarded if they apply management skills – of selection and/or timing.

The remainder of the individual stock risk is market related, but not

HOW TO COPE WITH RISK

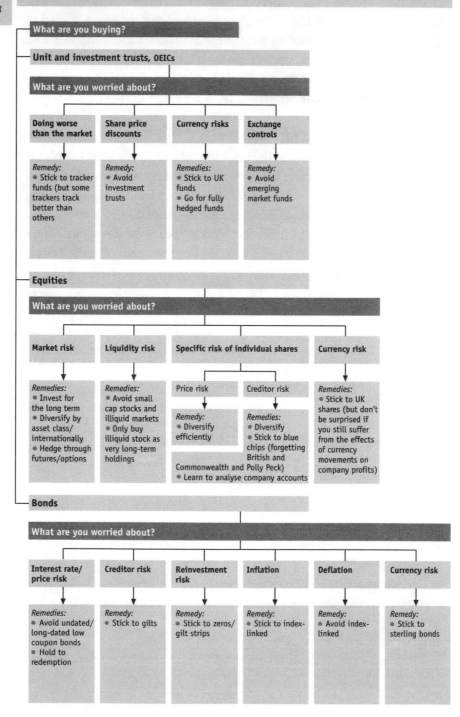

What are you buying?

Unit and investment trusts, OEICs

What are you worried about?

Doing worse than the market	Share price discounts	Currency risks	Exchange controls
Remedy: ● Stick to tracker funds (but some trackers track better than others	*Remedy:* ● Avoid investment trusts	*Remedies:* ● Stick to UK funds ● Go for fully hedged funds	*Remedy:* ● Avoid emerging market funds

Equities

What are you worried about?

Market risk	Liquidity risk	Specific risk of individual shares		Currency risk
Remedies: ● Invest for the long term ● Diversify by asset class/ internationally ● Hedge through futures/options	*Remedies:* ● Avoid small cap stocks and illiquid markets ● Only buy illiquid stock as very long-term holdings	Price risk *Remedy:* ● Diversify efficiently	Creditor risk *Remedies:* ● Diversify ● Stick to blue chips (forgetting British and Commonwealth and Polly Peck) ● Learn to analyse company accounts	*Remedies:* ● Stick to UK shares (but don't be surprised if you still suffer from the effects of currency movements on company profits)

Bonds

What are you worried about?

Interest rate/ price risk	Creditor risk	Reinvestment risk	Inflation	Deflation	Currency risk
Remedies: ● Avoid undated/ long-dated low coupon bonds ● Hold to redemption	*Remedy:* ● Stick to gilts	*Remedy:* ● Stick to zeros/ gilt strips	*Remedy:* ● Stick to index-linked	*Remedy:* ● Avoid index-linked	*Remedy:* ● Stick to sterling bonds

on a one-for-one basis. Some shares are cyclical, like those of banks and chemicals, and they vary in price by more than the broad indices do. They are said to have a high beta; an average share will have a beta of one, but some have historical betas of as much as 1.5 and are therefore attractive to hold in a bull market. Other kinds of companies such as pharmaceuticals or utilities are likely to have betas of less than one, and so can be regarded as defensive.

Risk, as mathematically defined, is symmetrical, but investors naturally regard upside risk very differently from downside risk. These days investors are often recommended to accept the risks of the stock market because the rewards in terms of extra returns have been very high during the past twenty years. The upside risks have been overwhelmingly in evidence. In the very long term, however, the extra returns on equities are only secured if investors stay invested even in the worst times, such as 1932 or 1974 (by the standards of those years 1987 was only a mild setback).

A common mistake of amateur investors is to be frightened out of stocks during a bear market and then miss the initial upturn, which is normally very sharp. If you cannot keep your nerve, you should steer clear of volatile investments.

It may seem too risky to stay in; but perhaps it is also very risky to be out.

CAUTIONARY TALES

Gearing's two faces

Anyone who has bought a house using a mortgage will understand the principle of gearing. Putting down a small amount of your own money entitles you to a property worth considerably more, the balance being provided by the mortgage company, using the house itself as collateral.

If prices have risen when you sell, your percentage profit will be considerably more than the percentage rise in value of the house. Say you put down £10,000 on a £100,000 house and sell it for £160,000, without paying off any of your mortgage meanwhile. The price of the house has risen by 60 per cent, but the value of your 'equity' in the house is now £70,000 (£10,000 deposit plus £60,000 profit) – seven times your initial 'investment'. But, if house prices fall, your debt is constant, and you could end up with 'negative equity' – a house worth less than your mortgage.

The same thing happens in the stock market. In the run-up to the 1929 crash on Wall Street speculators made fortunes trading on 'margin'. They bought shares by depositing a small proportion of the purchase price in cash with their broker, and borrowing the rest from him using other securities as collateral.

As long as the stock market continued to rise, the speculators got disproportionately richer. And it did continue to rise because they were all buying. But when its direction changed, many of the speculators were ruined before they even had time to do the sums. The greater the degree of gearing, the greater the potential rewards – and the greater the risk.

Nowadays highly geared investments take different forms. The modern equivalents of those 1920s speculators are hedge funds such as Long-Term Capital Management, the US fund that nearly collapsed in September 1998.

HOW THE FT CAN HELP

Volatility ratings

Unit Trusts

Volatility is a measure of the riskiness of a security that shows how much its price bounces around. Weekend Money gives you two sets of volatility yardsticks every Saturday.

The page of **unit** and **investment trust statistics** shows volatility for individual trusts and sectors, and compares the averages for both kinds of trust with those on other assets. The **table of gilts** earlier in the section provides volatility figures for a selection of stocks.

The volatility figures on the trusts page are based on a statistical measure known as 'standard deviation'. The higher the figure, the more the price will fluctuate. As explained above, bank and building society deposits have zero volatility, since capital values do not fluctuate. The average unit and investment trusts, though, are both more volatile than the FTSE All-Share index – the proxy for the UK stock market as a whole. The market's volatility was 3.3 at the time we checked, while the average unit and investment trusts showed 4.1 and 5.8 respectively. Yet the returns provided by the trusts are lower – partly because of costs – than those theoretically available from the index. The theory that high risks are balanced by high rewards obviously has some limitations in practice.

The detailed figures on the rest of the page show big variations in volatility between different types of trust. In unit trusts, UK Gilts (1.2)

UNIT TRUSTS

Tables show the result of investing £1,000 over different time periods. Trusts are ranked on 3-

Indices	1 year (£)	3	5	10	Volatility	Yld%
Average Unit Trust	934	1185	1438	2687	4.1	2.5
Average Investment Trust	1006	1211	1512	3065	5.8	4.4
Bank	1045	1122	1207	1776	0.0	5.7
Building Society	1042	1113	1203	1773	0.0	5.4
Stockmarket: FTSE All-Share	1073	1527	1922	3746	3.3	3.3
Inflation	1033	1092	1159	1517	0.3	-

UK Growth	1 year (£)	3	5	10	Volatility	Yld%
Johnson Fry Slater Growth	982	1821	2188	4225	4.3	1.8
River & Mercantile 1st Growth	1110	1757	2227	-	3.4	1.4

and Fixed Interest (1.4) are the most stable. Unsurprisingly Global Emerging Markets (7.9) and Far East excluding Japan (8.3) are at the other end of the scale.

The only investment trust shares that offer low risk are zero-dividend preference shares of split-capital investment trusts, which have volatility of just 1.4. The capital shares belonging to these trusts are a much hairier proposition, with an average volatility of 9. Pity the poor investor who confuses the two.

Some trust analysts argue that a yardstick called 'drawdown' is more helpful than standard deviation. Drawdown measures the biggest price fall recorded over a three-year period, rather than the average fluctuations. It gives investors an idea of the most they stand to lose over a short period of time. But even drawdown is only useful if the future resembles the past – which sadly it often does not.

Our Saturday table of gilts publishes volatility figures based on something known as 'modified duration'. This measures the sensitivity of the stock price to changes in yield. Broadly, the longer the gilt has left to run to redemption, and the lower its coupon (its nominal interest rate), the more volatile it will be.

The modified duration number provides a good estimate of the percentage change in price resulting from a one percentage point change in the yield for a gilt of that maturity. Thus, if base rates fall by one percentage point, from 7 to 6 per cent, there would probably be an increase of less than 1 per cent in the price of a very short-dated gilt whereas prices of long-dated gilts would increase substantially.

Undated stocks are very volatile. And any gilt strip (where the whole of the return comes in the form of capital gain) will be more volatile than a conventional stock with the same redemption date.

TOP TIP

Biotech stocks

Few people are brave enough to invest in biotechnology stocks. And 1998's horror story from British Biotech, the bellwether of the sector, is hardly likely to have increased their numbers. Biotech shares have a history of violent swings: the sector as a whole comes in and out of investor fashion like a yo-yo. And individual shares can fall by 60 or 70 per cent virtually overnight when tests on a much hyped wonder drug prove disappointing.

Biotechnology is unlike most other sectors. First, it is hard for most people to understand what the companies are doing: the world of antibody receptors and killer-cell stimulation is tough going, even for science graduates. Second, biotechnology company finances come from a looking-glass world. Companies do not have profits, earnings or dividends. So there are no p/e ratios or yields to compare them with. Sales are often negligible as losses pile up for years at a time. And the favourite statistic is the 'burn rate' – how rapidly the company is burning up money – which allows you to calculate how long it will be before it sends round the begging bowl again. What's more, management is too often in the hands of enthusiastic scientists, who find it impossible to be objective about their company's prospects. 'When you move from the lab to the City, you need totally different people with hard-nosed, critical faculties,' argued one analyst.

Not deterred yet? Analysts have some rules of thumb for would-be investors.

● Focus on management skills, such as the record of the directors. Ignore the hype about possible scientific breakthroughs.
● Think twice before selling on bad news. Biotech shares tend to over-react in both directions. So there is often a bounce back after a big fall.
● Buying just ahead of important news is particularly risky. Press comment tends to increase and the shares can get very toppy in anticipation of successful results.
● Buy a broad spread of shares to reduce risk, and invest for the long term. The very long term.

Putting theory into practice

The mix of investments you choose to put your money into can provide a powerful defence against excessive losses if things go wrong. But what you select also depends on the kind of investor you are and the amount of time you want to spend finding the best returns

Certain kinds of investments, we know, are not for widows and orphans – being representatives of insecure investors who are of modest means and require regular income from their investments to get by.

But how are we to decide on an appropriate portfolio strategy for our own requirements?

On one side of the balance sheets as it were, we have to work out the liquidity, the income and the riskiness of capital values that are appropriate and tolerable for our personal situation; and, on the other, the optimum spread of assets that is likely to deliver the best combination of risk and return in the circumstances.

Modern portfolio theory (MPT) goes back to a revolutionary academic paper published by Harry Markowitz in 1952. The concepts were developed by other American financial theorists such as William Sharpe in the 1950s and 1960s.

Markowitz's main achievement was to work out the theory of portfolio selection. Different securities have various expected returns and risks that can be calculated from historical observations so long as these characteristics can be assumed to be stable over time.

Efficient portfolios were defined by Markowitz as those combining different securities in proportions that provide the best trade-offs between risk and return. If, on the other hand, you put together an *inefficient* portfolio you may end up with lower returns without any significant reduction in risk.

Professional investors often talk about the 'efficient frontier' – which is a curved line plotted on a chart of expected return against standard deviation. Portfolios along the frontier are all efficient; the investor has to select the portfolio that best meets his or her risk criteria.

The theory can embrace balanced investment strategies. Risky equities can be combined with less risky fixed-interest bonds and with risk-free liquidity to provide a much less risky overall portfolio.

Alternatively, risk-seeking investors can use negative liquidity (that is, they can borrow) in order to open up higher-return possibilities.

Later, Sharpe and others launched the Capital Asset Pricing Model, a simple formula linking risk and return for investments. The CAPM says that, in the equity market, the expected return on a particular stock over and above the risk-free rate is proportional to its sensitivity to market risk (that is, its beta coefficient).

A risky stock with a beta of 1.5 will therefore deliver 1.5 times the expected market return premium compared with risk-free Treasury bills (over many decades in the UK this extra market return has averaged some six percentage points a year). A defensive stock with a beta of 0.5 will generate only half the risk premium, however.

So should we seek to enjoy the high returns from holding volatile stocks? Only if we can accept the risk, and so long as we have some reason to believe that we have special knowledge. If all investors have the same information about stocks, and the same attitude to risk, they should logically all hold the same overall market portfolio.

Out of this 'efficient market hypothesis' the first index funds developed some twenty-five years ago in the US: these are low-cost funds that track general market indices, and because of their excellent performance they have become tremendously popular.

These various elements of modern portfolio theory are widely used by professional investors as the basis for the design of portfolios and the control of risks: the beta and tracking error of a portfolio can be calculated and fine-tuned, for example.

For personal investors, of course, the technicalities make the direct and rigorous application of MPT impractical. But there are some general conclusions to be drawn. Thus the unavoidable risks of equities can be diluted by including them in a broader portfolio that also includes fixed-income securities and bank deposits.

Most people are well advised to hold equities in the form of index funds, which expose them only to general market risk and not to specific stock risks that must be carefully managed. Keen and confident investors may nevertheless be ambitious enough to believe they can beat the market.

But only a concentrated portfolio of, say, ten or a dozen stocks will be small enough to generate high returns if all goes reasonably well. A portfolio of even, say, twenty securities will be quite highly diversified, unless it is narrowly focused on particular sectors.

Risk analysis can also be applied to investment funds. Many of them will carry close to market risk. However, aggressive growth funds will probably be risky, and so may highly specialist funds.

In international terms, emerging markets funds are especially volatile, as we have seen recently on the downside. True global funds, however, should be well diversified across many different stock markets, and may well be significantly less volatile than UK equity funds.

Investors seeking high risks and returns might do better to gear up index-fund investments through borrowings than to try to outguess the market on individual stocks or specialist funds. Statistically speaking this leveraging is likely to pay off eventually, but nothing can be guaranteed: the long-term statistical rule will only hold good if the investor can hold out through bad times.

Often, in practice, such investors will lose either their nerve or their creditworthiness as the market crumbles. Forced sales by leveraged speculators whose credit has been called in was a key element of the global stock market's weakness during 1998.

What about the other side of the investment equation, the setting of investment targets and the selection of risk levels? Risk tolerance is partly a question of personal temperament: whether you can actually sleep at night when your favourite shares are going through a bad patch.

But there are also practical issues of individual circumstances and life cycle. The central principle, again, is that risk investments can only be relied upon to pay off over the long run. So the shorter your investment

HOW TO IDENTIFY ROUNDABOUTS AND SWINGS

Some assets tend to move in the same direction at the same time; others do not even move in contrary directions. The former have a high 'correlation'; the latter a low or negative correlation. The well-diversified portfolio contains assets which have low correlation. This diagram shows correlations for UK assets, adjusted for inflation, over the period 1983–97. The lower the percentage figure, the lower the correlation. Thus there should be diversification benefits from combining cash with index-linked gilts, but few from combining equities with gilts and even fewer from combining conventional index-linked gilts.

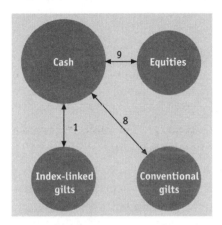

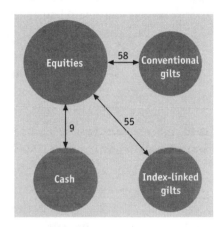

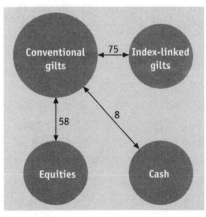

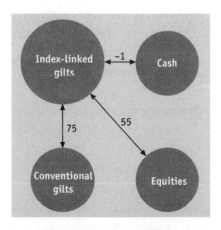

Figures are per cent

Warning
These are historical figures, not forecasts. Typical relationships do not always hold, and may change over time. In 1998, for example, gilts and equities have moved in different directions

Source for statistics: Barclays Capital

time horizon the more moderate the risks of your portfolio should be.

This is partly a simple question of age: old people should progressively switch to safe, income-producing assets. But younger people, too, may have short-term financial constraints which must be planned for, including school fees, house purchase and life's occasional big hazards such as divorce or redundancy.

There is a particularly large degree of controversy within the investment community about the risks in personal pension plans. Similar problems also apply to the increasingly common 'defined contribution' occupational pension schemes that devolve the investment risks on to individual scheme members.

In the artificially tax-constrained framework of a pension plan, the age-related risks of investments are especially important. Younger people in their thirties and forties can happily invest their plans in risky equities. But older people have to prepare to buy an annuity from a life assurance company at the age of, say, sixty. This implies a forced switch from equities to gilts (annuities are based on gilts).

To stay in equities until the very last minute in order to enjoy the last of the capital gains would be to risk the fate of some ill-prepared people retiring in summer 1998: between July and September the annuity which could be bought with a UK equity fund by a 65-year-old tumbled by some 25 per cent, because gilts and equities suddenly moved in opposite directions. Accordingly, much work has been done on automatic age-related risk-reduction programmes. Alternatively, drawdown annuities permit the switch out of equities to be phased over a number of years. But there are still serious risks that the timing decisions for drawdowns could turn out to be wrong.

In recent years the connection between high returns and high risks has seemed blurred: in a long bull market the risks have seemed only to be apparent on the upside. Now the long-term laws of risk and return are being reasserted. But the well-adjusted investor should not be unduly concerned. Portfolio theory makes it clear that, in the long run, it is almost as bad to accept too *little* risk as too much.

MPT is bunk

Modern portfolio theory has some illustrious opponents. Warren Buffett, the outstandingly successful American investor, has no time for MPT or most other academic investment theories.

He argues that all finance classes do is teach you to be average. Their only use is to tie the hands of other investment managers, making it even easier for him to run rings round them.

Berkshire Hathaway, his own investment company, has flourished by pursuing a contrariant strategy: taking very large positions in a small number of carefully selected companies – at the right price. And he argues that having a lumpy portfolio may, *pace* the academics, in practice reduce risk.

'We believe that a policy of portfolio concentration may well decrease risk if it raises, as it should do, both the intensity with which the investor thinks about a business and the comfort level he must feel with its economic characteristics before buying into it.'

That is a pretty hefty 'if'. One reason he only invests in a small number of companies is that very few meet his criteria.

'Your goal,' he says, 'is to purchase, at a rational price, a part interest in an easily understandable business whose earnings . . . are virtually certain to be materially higher five, ten and twenty years from now.'

What matters is not just that the companies continue to grow strongly, but that their ability to do so can be reliably predicted.

Buffett also warns against selling or trimming a successful holding merely because it bulks too large in a portfolio. After all, he says, do sports teams sell their stars?

This is all fine – if you are Warren Buffett. But are you confident of your ability to emulate him?

Yield indices

Many investors yearn for a patent way of picking portfolios of shares. One perennial favourite is concentrating on shares with an above-average yield. And, within the FTSE Actuaries share indices, one index includes shares with an above-average yield and one shares with a below-average yield. These are published in the table of FTSE Actuaries share indices, which appears on the back of the second section of the *FT* on Monday to Friday and in the first section on Saturdays.

FTSE Actuaries Share Indices					
Produced in conjunction with the Faculty and In				he UK	
	Sep 24	Day's chge%	Gross yield%	N yiel	P/E ratio	Xd y
FTSE 100	5167.6	−0.9	3.10	2	20.15	117
FTSE 250	4580.3	+0.4	3.91	3	15.39	10
FTSE 250 ex Inv Tr	4623.5	+0.3	4.06	3	14.39	110
FTSE 350	2464.1	−0.7	3.24	2	19.15	56
FTSE 350 ex Inv Tr	2470.7	−0.7	3.25	2	18.95	5
FTSE 350 Higher Yield	2371.5	−1.1	4.36	3	14.74	70
FTSE 350 Lower Yield	2556.5	−0.2	2.06	1	28.00	44
FTSE SmallCap	2032.78	......	4.03	3	16.38	46
FTSE SmallCap ex Inv Tr	2021.35	−0.1	4.31	3	14.63	48
FTSE All-Share	2388.23	−0.7	3.28	2	18.98	54
					18.70	5

The two indices divide the 350 largest companies in the UK according to their dividend yields. In the example shown here, the dividend yield on the **Higher Yield** index was roughly double that on its **Lower Yield** rival, while the p/e ratio was roughly half.

That is not surprising. Companies normally have relatively high yields because investors expect their share prices to perform relatively badly. There are three main types of high yielder: stodgy companies, such as utilities (in theory anyway), that chug along but never produce fireworks; companies in decline that are overdistributing, since there is no reason to invest new money in a dying business; and recovery shares that may – or may not – make it back. Since p/e ratios reflect growth expectations, a bunch of laggards and walking wounded is unlikely to have a high ratio. In strong contrast, the Low Yield index comprises the market's darlings, companies that are expected to streak ahead of the pack for one reason or another. In the past, however, high-yield shares have often played tortoise and beaten their seemingly fleeter rivals. Investment gurus, from Benjamin Graham onwards, have argued that high yield, when supported by other filters, is a good way to pick shares offering good fundamental value. Others have used such criteria to select portfolios mechanically. The argument is that, although buying individual high-yield shares is risky, buying a portfolio of several reduces the risk to acceptable proportions, leaving the investor with the hope of above-average returns on the portfolio as a whole.

But the high-yield system seems to have run out of road – at least for the time being. Since its launch, the Low Yield index has handsomely outperformed the High Yield one. There are several possible explanations for this.

• Yield-based systems are a form of bargain hunting, and there are more bargains around when the market is bumping around the bottom. Value investing and high-yield shares will come into their own again if and when the market has a serious fall and a recession pulls more companies to their knees.

• Yield-based systems were fine when stock market analysis involved laborious calculations which few could be bothered to do. Nowadays an analyst can search the market for high-yield stocks with a single click of a computer button. So anomalies do not last long.

• High-yield investment theories have become very popular. All investment theories cease to work when they become part of common wisdom. But the indices remain useful yardsticks for checking out possible additions to your portfolio, whichever school – growth or value – you belong to.

TOP TIP

Tracker funds

Professional investors have long used index-tracking funds as the core of their investment portfolios. In the US, the Vanguard group, which pioneered the concept among retail investors, has for years enjoyed a strong following. But few individual UK investors had heard of them until Richard Branson popularized the concept with the Virgin PEP. Unless you are certain you can pick an actively managed fund that will beat the market consistently, trackers are well worth considering.

An index-tracking unit trust is one that aims to reproduce the performance of a stock market index, such as the FTSE 100 or the All-Share index, not to beat it. Trackers, also known as passive funds, are cheap to run, because management consists of following a computer programme with no expensive investment experts to pay. Conventional active funds employ highly paid managers in an attempt to beat the index. Often they fail. But, even if they succeed, their higher costs often mean that the net result to the investor is little better.

Whereas conventional unit trusts often have initial charges of 3–5 per cent, and annual fees of 1–1.5 per cent, most trackers have no initial charge and annual charges as low as 0.35 per cent. So the return to the investor is only slightly below that on the index.

Tracker fans argue that fund managers in aggregate cannot beat the market – since they are the market. Most of those that show an outstanding performance at any given time tend to revert to the average after a few years. And even the handful that do produce consistently sparkling results are hard to identify in advance.

Points to check when choosing a tracker include

● What index is it tracking? Most analysts recommend a broad-based index, such as the All-Share for the long haul, and certainly not one of the more specialized ones.

- How big is the fund? The bigger the fund, the easier it is for it to track accurately and keep its costs down.
- What are its costs? Virgin's may be best known; it is not the cheapest.

Market efficiency and the random walk

Efficient-market theorists argue that stock markets automatically follow the publicly available information about a company. As a result, they say, active-fund managers will seldom outperform tracker funds. Fund managers, of course, disagree

Mobile telephones are all the rage. Everyone on the train seems to have one, characters on TV use them all the time and their popularity prompts features in colour supplements.

So this is the time to rush out and buy shares in mobile telephone companies, right? Wrong, according to efficient market theory.

The theory states that share prices should have already moved to reflect the promising fundamentals for the telecommunications groups. Their sales growth appears in their annual accounts, and in trading statements; analysts will have adjusted their profit forecasts to take account of the companies' growth prospects; and the investment institutions will have taken note and bought the stocks. By the time a trend gets noticed in the colour supplements, smart investors will have taken note long ago.

The stock market is thus 'efficient', and this term has nothing to do with whether your stockbroker answers the phone promptly or sends a cheque for the right amount when you sell shares.

An efficient market is one in which the price of a commodity (which can be anything from a share price to pork bellies) reflects all the publicly available information about the product.

The only thing that should affect the price in future, therefore, is genuine 'news' which, by definition, cannot be known in advance. It is theoretically possible, of course, to have information about a company or product that is not publicly known, such as an impending takeover, but the chances are that you will then be indulging in insider dealing.

Efficient-market theorists argue that share prices should follow a 'random walk' rather like the progress of a drunk after pub closing time, in which the direction of each successive step cannot be predicted by observing the preceding paces.

What evidence is there that efficient-market theory is correct? One good pointer is the recent success of index funds relative to the active-fund managers, who spend their time poring over balance sheets, interviewing managements and crunching numbers.

For example, over the five years to 1 September 1998, only eight out of 108 UK growth and income unit trusts managed to beat the HSBC Footsie fund, which simply buys and holds the stocks in the FTSE 100 index. All the efforts of the active-fund managers are simply not worth the fees that investors pay them; past research has shown that 80 per cent regularly fail to beat the benchmark.

As one might expect, the fund management industry has not taken this argument lying down. The theoretical counter-attack has come from a number of directions:

● Statistics that show managers underperforming the index are misleading. For a start, an index is a theoretical construct that does not allow for dealing costs or fees. Those costs give managers an immediate handicap when they try to outperform, and, since even tracker funds incur costs, they too tend to underperform the index – albeit only marginally.

Second, the index represents the collective portfolios of all investors and thus is a measure of the average performance of those investors. If the index is the average, but the index has no costs, it is small wonder that the average fund manager fails to beat it.

● Whatever efficient-market theorists suggest, there are fund managers who have been consistently able to outperform the market, such as Warren Buffett or George Soros.

● Market studies have thrown up a series of anomalies that contradict the efficient-market theory. For example, share prices tend to do better in January than at other times of the year and strategies such as buying high-yield, or low-price/earnings-ratio stocks tend to outperform over the long run.

• Merely observing the market seems to throw up times when it is a long way from efficiency. Could corporate America really have been worth 22 per cent less the day after Black Monday – 19 October 1987? Bubbles do appear to develop in asset markets. And, if a bubble has developed in recent years, tracking funds, which blindly buy stocks just because they are part of the index, may bear part of the blame.

The standard story told by active-fund managers is of the efficient-market theorist, who is walking along a street, when he sees a £10 note on the ground. 'That note cannot really be there,' reasons the theorist, 'because if it were, someone would have spotted it before me and picked it up.' So the sage ignores the money and keeps on walking.

• In the real world, information is not instantly available to all investors. Some insiders are 'in the loop' (albeit at some times illegally so), and this can give them an advantage.

• Chartists, or technical analysts, argue that markets are governed by the psychological reactions of investors and it is possible to analyse those factors by looking at price patterns.

Fans of the efficient-market theory, and of index funds, have responded to these points. On the Buffett/Soros argument, they accept that certain managers have outperformed over time. But they argue that this does no more than confirm the laws of probability.

Were the UK population to indulge in a coin-tossing competition, with those throwing a head proceeding to the next round, roughly half of the contestants would be eliminated each time. After about seventeen rounds, you would have around 400 remaining contestants. Each would no doubt be convinced of his or her coin-tossing skills and would give press interviews detailing the wrist action involved. And yet, in reality, their chances of tossing heads next time would remain 50–50.

Buffett and Soros are, in any case, very much the exceptions that prove the rule. Pension and mutual-fund managers show the ability to beat the market over short periods, but the vast majority fail to do so over long periods of time.

On the question of market anomalies, the efficient-market theorists have been forced to retreat a little. So-called 'weak' efficient-market theory accepts that some anomalies can occur, but says that they can

ARE YOU AN EFFICIENT MARKETEER?

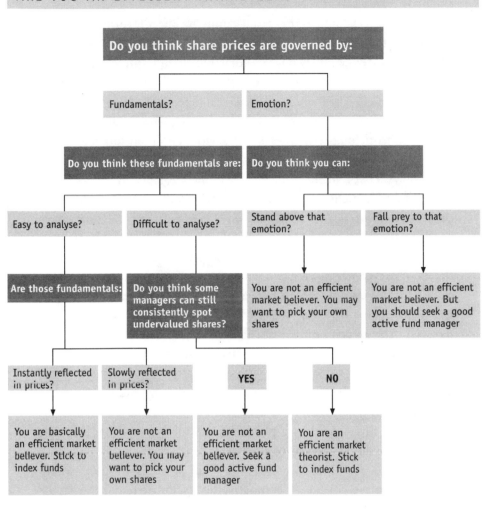

58

only be recognized in retrospect and will disappear if everyone tries to exploit them.

A real-world example is the 'small-company effect', trumpeted in the late 1980s, that showed that small companies tended to outperform over time. Since then, they have steadfastly tended to underperform.

And wild swings in prices are not necessarily incompatible with efficient markets. The theoretical value of a share is the discounted value of all future dividends; the discount rate applied to such dividends will be derived from long-term interest rates with a risk premium added.

A sudden event, such as an unexpected increase in interest rates, would have a twofold effect on the discount rate, since investors might well demand a higher risk premium. The result could be a dramatic drop in the theoretical value of the shares. Some similar effect may have triggered the crash of 1987.

Whether or not one believes in the full-blown efficient-market theory – and plenty of people do not – it is still a pretty good rule of thumb for private investors. If a broker offers you a golden opportunity, it is worth asking why other people have not spotted it too; and if they have, why the golden future is not already reflected in the share price.

One of the most costly mistakes made by private investors is the constant churning of portfolios, with all the attendant dealing charges, and a belief in efficient-market theory should help individuals avoid this trap.

However, there could be a plausible case for arguing that different markets have different levels of efficiency.

The market for blue-chip stocks on Wall Street is an arena where legions of analysts cover each company, the disclosure requirements for companies are high and information is instantly available to investors via news wire services and financial television. As a result, it should be quite difficult to find obviously underpriced stocks, just as it is unlikely one would find an undiscovered old master at a Christie's auction.

In contrast, the market for, say, small companies in Thailand will be far less researched and it is more likely that some stocks will be under- (and of course over-) priced. Risks will be higher but you might, like the assiduous buyer at a car boot sale, find a bargain.

Sure enough, fund managers have found it much easier to beat the indices in emerging markets than they have in the developed bourses of the US and UK.

And even in the UK, it is possible to argue that the lack of coverage of smaller companies makes that area of the market less than efficient.

The ultimate irony could be that, if too many people believe in efficient markets, they will use index funds and stop analysing individual companies. In the long run, a widespread belief in efficient markets would make the markets inefficient.

PROFILE GEORGE SOROS

Lone raider

If you are looking for a powerful case against efficient-market theory, you need look no further than George Soros, the hedge-fund manager whose speculative raids have caused governments round the world to tremble.

Soros may make a lot of money out of free markets but he believes they can be inherently unstable. His theory of reflexivity, which he has outlined at length in books and speeches, tries to explain how market bubbles and crashes occur.

The reflexivity theory states that fundamentals and perceptions can get out of line in financial markets. Furthermore the fundamentals can actually be affected by those perceptions, leading to feedback loops that cause prices to move rapidly.

A good example of the theory is the relationship between banks and property prices. Many investors in property are using borrowed money, with the bank using the value of the property as collateral.

When property prices rise, the banks feel more confident about their collateral and are willing to lend more money; this means that investors have more funds to put into the property market pushing up prices even further. But, when banks lose confidence in the market, they become unwilling to lend and may call in previous loans. This forces property investors to sell, pushing down prices, reducing the value of the banks' collateral and sending the spiral in the other direction.

Given Soros's highly successful, although far from flawless, record in making money, one has to take his theory seriously. But it is not that easy to recognize when the reflexivity process is in operation, or whether the fundamentals are really changing; that may be a skill only Soros has.

HOW THE FT CAN HELP

Highs and lows

Buy low and sell high is the ultimate aim of all investors, but in the stock market, this can be a more complex business than it seems.

From Tuesday to Saturday, the *Financial Times* publishes a table of shares and gilts that have reached a 52-week high or low, **new 52-week highs and lows.** (Highs and lows for each individual share are printed on the London share service pages.) Note that these figures are based on intra-day, rather than closing, prices.

NEW 52 WEEK HIGHS AND LOWS

NEW HIGHS (51).
GILTS (38) Conv 9 1/2pc 2001, Conv 9 3/4pc 2003, Conversion 10pc 2002, Conversion 9 1/2 pc 2004, Conversion 9 1/2 pc 2005, Conversion 9 1/2pc 2002, Conversion 9 3/4pc 2006, Conversion 9pc Ln 2011, Exchequer 10 1/2pc 2005, Exchequer 12pc 2013–17, Exchequer 9pc 2002, Funding 3 1/2 pc 1999–2004, Treas 7 1/2pc 2006, Treas 6 1/2pc 2003, Treas 6 1/4pc 2010, Treas 6 3/4pc 2004, Treas 8pc 2028, Treas 7 1/4pc 2007, Treas 7 3/4pc 2006, Treas 7pc 2001, Treas 7pc 2002, Treas 8pc 2003, Treas 8pc 2013, Treasury 10pc 2003, Treasury 10pc 2004, Treasury 11 3/4 pc 2003 –07, Treasury 121/2 pc 2003–05, Treasury 13 1/2pc 2004–08, Treasury 5 1/2 pc 2008–12, Treasury 5 3/4pc 2009, Treasury 7 3/4 pc 2012–15, Treasury 8 1/2 pc 2007, Treasury 8 1/2pc 2005, Treasury 8pc 2000, Treasury 8pc 2002–06, Treasury 8pc 2009, Treasury 9 3/4 pc 2002, Treasury 9pc 2008, Treasury 9pc 2012, ELECTRICITY (2) Southern Electric, Viridian, GAS DISTRIBUTION (1) BG, INVESTMENT TRUSTS (6) Exeter Preferred Cap Zero Deb 2002, Foreign & Col Special Income, Henderson Geared Inc & Grth Zero Div Pref, INVESCO Gearded Opp's Zero Div, INVESCO Recovery Pfd Growth, Jos Hldgs Zero Div Pref, PROPERTY (1) British Land 8 7/8pc Deb 2035, TRANSPORT (1) Railtrack, AMERICANS (1) BellSouth Corpn.
NEW LOWS (337).
GILTS (4) Exchequer 12 1/4 pc 1999, Exchequer 12pc 1998, Exchequer 12pc 99–2002, Treasury 9 1/2 pc Ln. 1999, ALCOHOLIC BEVERAGES (1) Seagram, BANKS, RETAIL (13) ABN Amro Holdings, Asahi, Bank of Tokyo Mitsubishi Bk, Barclays, Deutsche Bank, Fuji Bank, Mitsubishi Trust & Banking, Mitsui Trust & Banking, Sakura Bank, Sanwa Bank,

Two stocks that have reached recent peaks or nadirs are highlighted in the graphs above the table.

One approach would be to look for bargains among the stocks that are at new lows and to take profits in those that have reached highs.

However, efficient-market theory tells us that these stocks have reached highs or lows for a reason. Stocks that are at new lows have usually seen a deterioration in their trading or financial position.

Though stocks can rise from the dead, some keep on falling all the way to suspension and wipe out of capital.

Similarly, just because a stock is at a new high does not mean that its rise is over. Microsoft, the US software group, has been reaching all-time share price highs for much of its history; selling at an early high would have been a big mistake.

Indeed a study by Jim O'Shaughnessy, which covered forty years of US stockmarket history, found that one of the most successful strategies was to buy the fifty shares that had performed best over the previous year, a case of 'buy high and sell higher'.

The table can also be used to glean information about the overall state of the stock market. First, the entries are broken down by sector. On 1 October 1998, for example, there were fifty-one new highs, but thirty-nine were gilts and six were specialist investment trust securities. Of the remainder, most were utility stocks, seen as defensive havens in a volatile market.

Among the 337 new lows, there was strong representation from conventional investment trusts (which are linked to the level of the market), and from cyclical sectors such as engineering.

Some technical analysts also use new highs and lows as a means of checking the underlying health of the market. They like an index high to be 'confirmed' by an increase in new highs, because that is an indication of a broad market rise. Similarly, if the number of new lows starts to diminish, that may be a sign that the index is close to bottoming.

Another indication of the breadth of the market can be found in a table that sits next to the highs and lows information **the rises and falls yesterday**. Again, technical analysts like to see an index increase accompanied by a surplus of rising over falling stocks. Some keep a cumulative total of daily rises and falls; early in 1998, that line started to tail off in the US market, even though the Dow Jones Industrial Average was still recording new peaks. In retrospect, some see that as a premonition of the trouble that was in store for Wall Street.

That table, too, is split by industrial groupings. The table for 1 October 1998, for example, shows that, on a bad day for the market, rising utility stocks outweighed fallers while, among investment trusts, losers outnumbered winners by seven to one.

Calendar reading

Sell in May and go away is one of the oldest bits of stock market lore, although the follow up (come back on St Leger day) is more normally forgotten.

Does the advice have any practical use? An investor would certainly have done well to pay attention in 1998; profit-taking in May would have left him or her well positioned by the time the market started to correct in mid July.

Figures from David Schwartz, the stock market historian, show that May and June are, on average, the worst two months of the year and September is the third worst (the St Leger tends to fall in early-to-mid September). Over the May to September period, investors barely made money over the long run.

One could postulate a number of reasons for this historical oddity: investors tend to be away during the summer, leading to lower liquidity; junior staff are left in charge of portfolios and are reluctant to make significant buying decisions; the summer tends to be the period when the rosy earnings forecasts made by analysts at the start of the year get revised downwards.

However, whether it is easy for the private investor to make a regular profit out of these anomalies is another matter. The average movement in most months is quite small; only one (January) has seen a consistent shift of more than 2 per cent in either direction. Attempts to time the market in such circumstances are likely to see any gains wiped out by dealing costs.

And one has also to ask whether the differences between monthly performances represent anything other than the statistical randomness thrown up by the laws of probabilities.

Investing in months that have been profitable in the past may indeed be no more sensible than picking the most frequently occurring lottery numbers (or indeed the least frequently occurring).

Analysis of market fundamentals such as interest rates, price/earnings ratios and dividend yields might be far from flawless, but it would appear to be a more rational approach.

Markets or stocks: what kind of equity investor are you?

Inside some private investors there is a thrusting City trader aching to get out. Others prefer a quieter life studying figures and reading the small print. Understanding your own preferences is a crucial part of forging a sound investment strategy

There are nine and sixty ways of constructing tribal lays. And – every – single – one – of – them – is – right!

There is no template for the successful equity investor. Some concentrate on getting their market timing right: others are only interested in picking individual shares. Some start with the big economic picture and use this as the basis for deciding which types of business are likely to do well over the next few months: others pore over balance sheets or visit the local shopping centre hoping to spot unappreciated companies. Some buy and hold virtually for ever; others love 'em and leave 'em.

Some base their decisions on chart patterns that suggest what other investors are likely to do next; others consider such practices akin to reading the entrails of chickens. Some are adventurous optimists concentrating on a share's potential to rise in value; others are cautious folk worrying about how far it could fall.

We shall be examining some of the most popular techniques in the next few chapters in this book. But experimenting with every style in turn could be time-consuming and expensive. So in this chapter we provide some pointers to help you decide which methods might suit you.

This is partly a question of finding an approach that appeals to you. All great investors are hobbyists at heart: they enjoy what they do. But you also need to consider the practical side. Do you have the time to pursue your chosen method? It is no coincidence that many people become enthusiastic private investors after they have retired. If you do not have enough time in a busy working life, you should probably settle for having your money managed by a kindred spirit.

The other practical consideration is access to information. Professional fund managers who work for large organizations are surrounded by screens providing on-line prices and information, deafened by analysts summarizing their latest research report, and cordially welcomed by most companies if they want to visit. Private investors cannot afford the pricey machines, and are unlikely to get the red-carpet treatment from analysts or companies. So think hard before choosing an investment approach that involves pitting your wits against the pros, without having comparable resources.

● **The top-down approach.** This is for people who believe that the world is a logical place and see investment analysis as a funnel. Start with the economic outlook for Britain – and indeed the world. Decide points such as where we are in the business cycle and what is likely to happen to currency and interest rates and inflation. Take a view on bonds and equities. Make or adjust your overall 'asset allocation' accordingly – what proportions of your total portfolio you have in bonds, shares and cash and in which countries? Check whether this broad split appears to conform to the principles of modern portfolio management theory.

Then do your sector selection. Your normal UK portfolio weightings are probably broadly modelled on the FTSE All-Share index anyway. So all you are doing is fine-tuning. Is the looming recession likely to be bad news for construction shares? In that case perhaps you should reduce your holdings in the construction sector and increase your stake in debt collectors. Then check whether the market ratings of construction shares are already allowing/more than allowing for the probable downturn. And finally have a glance at the relative ratings of the main construction companies to decide whether/where to go over/underweight.

If this approach appeals to you, you were born to be a conventional fund manager – or perhaps an equity strategist. But there is no point in trying to run a personal portfolio in this way. You do not have enough money or equipment.

Tips. Put your money into unit and investment trusts. If you are a realist, go for a tracker fund. If you still aspire to beat the market, choose a group where analyst Fund Research reckons the management has a sound top-down investment process.

• **Market-timing.** Getting in and out of markets at the right time can pay handsomely. The PDFM study of total returns on different types of securities shows that any investor who put his entire portfolio into the best performing sector (gilts, UK equities, etc) at the start of each calendar year for the last thirty-five years, would have notched up average returns of 28 per cent a year, double those of someone who kept the lot in UK equities throughout.

But it is a tall order. In the next chapter we shall discuss a number of mechanical systems used to predict market turning points. But remember, if any of them worked perfectly, everyone would adopt them and they would cease to work.

Tips. Read Charles Kindleberger on *Manias, Panics and Crashes*, George Soros on *The Alchemy of Finance* and David Charters' primer on technical analysis *Charters on Charting*.

• **Trading.** Traders are out to make a quick buck by buying cheap and selling dear. They do not much mind what they are dealing in, and pros sometimes hold a stock for a remarkably short time. They resemble market timers but operate on a much shorter timescale.

Some traders rely on fundamental analysis to spot anomalies when purchasing, but snatching your profits may still depend on split-second timing. And this is possible only if you have instant access to information, through a system such as Market Eye.

Private investors who fancy themselves in red braces should also look at the costs. Higher dealing charges and spreads mean that a private investor may fail to make money doing a trade that would be profitable for his professional counterpart.

Tips. Read Soros and Charters as before. Alternatively, lie down until the urge goes away.

• **Stockpicking.** Some of the best individual fund managers are stockpickers with little time for strategic asset allocation. They simply look for companies they like or shares that are undervalued, or preferably the two combined, and ignore the stock market's fluctuations.

The US, where successful investors are national heroes, has lots of

CHECK OUT YOUR NATURAL AFFINITIES

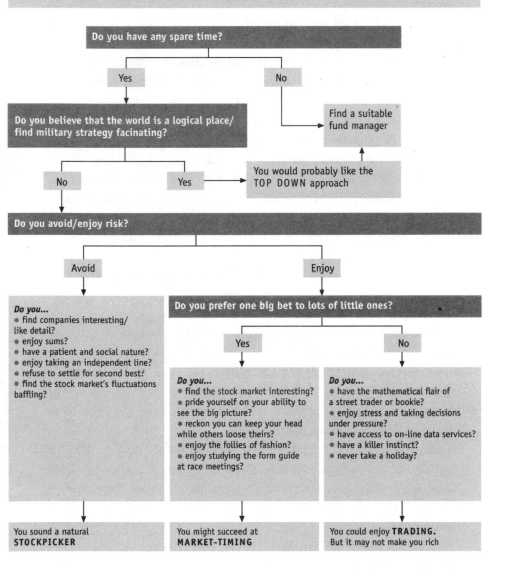

Do you have any spare time?

Yes → Do you believe that the world is a logical place/ find military strategy facinating?

No → Find a suitable fund manager

No → **Do you avoid/enjoy risk?**

Yes → You would probably like the TOP DOWN approach → Find a suitable fund manager

Do you avoid/enjoy risk?

Avoid → Do you...
• find companies interesting/ like detail?
• enjoy sums?
• have a patient and social nature?
• enjoy taking an independent line?
• refuse to settle for second best?
• find the stock market's fluctuations baffling?

→ You sound a natural **STOCKPICKER**

Enjoy → **Do you prefer one big bet to lots of little ones?**

Yes → Do you...
• find the stock market interesting?
• pride yourself on your ability to see the big picture?
• reckon you can keep your head while others loose theirs?
• enjoy the follies of fashion?
• enjoy studying the form guide at race meetings?

→ You might succeed at **MARKET-TIMING**

No → Do you...
• have the mathematical flair of a street trader or bookie?
• enjoy stress and taking decisions under pressure?
• have access to on-line data services?
• have a killer instinct?
• never take a holiday?

→ You could enjoy **TRADING**. But it may not make you rich

different stockpickers to emulate: Benjamin Graham, who invented investment analysis, Warren Buffett (Graham's best known disciple), T. Rowe Price, the first man to search for growth shares systematically, Peter Lynch, who ran the mighty Magellan fund in its glory days. Lynch worked for fund management group Fidelity, which has long been unusual in giving its fund managers a lot of freedom. And it is no accident that one of Britain's best known stockpickers, Anthony Bolton, runs European funds for Fidelity.

But the fact that they all concentrate on picking stocks does not mean that they all use the same selection method, run the same types of port-folio, or hold the shares for the same length of time. Some follow a 'buy and hold' strategy: be very selective in picking companies to invest in, but hang on to the shares once you have got them. Others are more cold-hearted: they have a price target in mind when they buy, and sell when the share price reaches it.

The conventional distinction is between investors searching for value – shares whose existing attractions are underrated – and investors searching for growth – shares that may well look expensive on past performance, but have enormous long-term growth potential. We shall be considering the difference in a future chapter.

As a crude generalization, value investors tend to like crunching numbers and reading the small print in company accounts. They are meticulous people who do not like taking risks and look at the downside before considering the upside.

Growth investors can usually do sums too if they have to. But they are natural enthusiasts who love discovering new themes and hidden gems first. They concentrate on the upside, and can sometimes be found taking their children shopping so that they can spot the hot new trends.

A few successful stockpickers – such as Peter Lynch – use a number of different approaches when picking shares. And what they expect of a share and how they treat it after purchase will depend on which category it falls into. But most discover an affinity for a specific type.

Many stockpickers gravitate towards smaller companies, with good reason. Many professional investors and analysts have a high cut-off level, so there are likely to be more neglected shares among smaller companies. But one of Warren Buffett's favourite holdings is Coca-Cola, no minnow.

Note that most successful professional stockpickers had extensive experience working for traditional investment firms before they evolved their patent formulas. This gave them time to find out what worked and what they were good at, and make their mistakes with someone else's money.

It is hard for a private investor to replicate this experience. But the more background work you do before you start putting your own money where your mouth is, the better.

Tips. Read Benjamin Graham's *The Intelligent Investor*, and John Train's *The Money Masters*.

INVESTMENT ANALYSIS

Chartists

Chartists, or technical analysts to give them their proper name, are investment analysts who predict future price movements by studying charts of past price movements.

Charts are used to analyse price prospects for whole stock markets, individual shares, groups of shares, currencies, commodities and interest rates. Some investors scorn charting; some rely on it exclusively; many treat it as a useful adjunct to fundamental analysis.

A company and its share price are two different things. The fundamentalist studies a company's business, history and prospects to work out where he thinks its price 'ought' to be. A chartist looks at the price and where it is likely to go next.

Chartists argue that what matters in markets is the balance between supply and demand, and that this is reflected accurately in investors' purchases and sales of shares. The study of a number of charts shows certain recurring patterns. If X happens, Y often follows. So charting may be a better guide to what is likely to happen to a share price than analysing the company's business.

The basic techniques of modern stock-market charting were developed in the West by Charles Dow (the man behind the Dow Jones Average). But the Japanese had been using what are called 'candlestick' charts centuries earlier in the rice trade. And candlesticks are popular with many stock-market investors today.

Charting is mainly concerned with investment timing, not investment choice, which is why it is popular with market timers and traders. Most currency trading desks employ a chartist.

Chartists accept that they will never catch a share or market right at the top or bottom. What they aim to do is catch it soon after it has bottomed, run their profits as long as it is safe, and sell it soon after its peak.

HOW THE FT CAN HELP

Stock classifications

Many safety-first investors are interested only in big companies. Contrariwise, many private stockpickers concentrate on small companies. The *FT* publishes a number of stock market indices, covering companies of varying sizes. The main ones are the FTSE 100 index, the FTSE 250 index, and the FTSE SmallCap index.

TRADING VOLUME

■ Major Stocks yesterday.

	Vol 000's	Closing price	Day's change
3i	1,100	500	–5
AMVESCAP	3,000	303	–34¼
ASDA Group	12,600	173	+1¼
Abbey National	4,700	944	–70
Alliance & Leicester	2,200	868	–3
Allied Domecq	2,700	400	–25
Allied Zurich	5,400	542½	–59½
Anglian Water†	899	948½	+½
Assoc. Brit. Foods	1,600	571	–28½
BAA	2,800	598	–1½
BOC	2,500	719	–11
BG	13,700	405	–4
BP	19,900	856	–44
BSkyB	3,800	493	–8
BT	10,400	778	–15
BTR	4,700	105¾	–½
Bank of Scotland	8,100	521	–40½

AIM

For A de Gruchy see under Retailers General

AFA Systems		120½	......	191	74½
AMCO		95xd	......	136½	93½
ATA	Z	133½	–½	157½	132½
AdVal Group		47½	–1½	67½	47½
Access Plus	♣†	190	......	271	159
African Gold	♣g	3¼	......	8¼	3¼
Albemarle & Bond	♣	62½	......	96½	33½
Alizyme	♣	29½	......	43½	29½
Ambient Media		58	–½	102½	57½
Ambishus Pub Co	♣	132½	......	290	132½
Anglo Siberian Oil Co		101	......	108½	98½
Anglo-Welsh	♣	93½	......	119	72½
Antonov	♣	80	–6½	117½	74½
AorTech	♣	87	......	122½	87
Aram Resources	K	80	......	102	80
Archer Dedicated		65	......	90	50
Ask Central	†g	280	......	485	212¼
Atlantic Caspian		11¾	–¼	24¾	10
Avalon Oil		10	......	69½	9½
BATM Advanced Comms		159	–1	193	120½
BCO Technologies		178½	......	238½	148½
BGR	LW	180	......	317½	175

For BKG Resources see GTL Resources

The FTSE 100 index contains the top 100 companies on the London Stock Exchange – the so-called blue chips, and the only shares some big professional investors are interested in. They are listed in the **trading volume** table which appears on the back page of the second section of the paper on Tuesdays to Fridays, and inside the first section on Saturdays. Membership of the index is reviewed every quarter, and there is a reserve list of companies that might be upgraded at the next change. These companies are also included in the trading volume table, marked with a dagger (†).

The FTSE 250 index covers the second tier. The market capitalization figures given in the Monday share service (see page 32) are a useful pointer to which companies might qualify for inclusion – although the cut-off points between the different indices inevitably vary with the market level. When, for example, the FTSE 100 index was around 5,250 at the end of August 1998, the border between the bottom of the 100 and the top of the 250 index came at a market cap of around £2.3bn. At the same time, the border between the bottom of the 250 and the top of the SmallCap index came at about £250m. And the SmallCap gave way to the Fledgling index at a market cap of around £35m.

But these are very rough yardsticks indeed. For, in between the quarterly reviews, movements in the prices of individual shares can leave many anomalies.

The FT share service lists companies traded on the **Alternative Investment Market** (AIM) in a separate category at the end of the second page. This separation reflects the less rigorous criteria applied to AIM stocks. Whereas companies joining the main market are vetted by the Stock Exchange itself – those joining AIM have lower standards to meet and are vetted by their own adviser. Few brokers research AIM stocks and the shares may be harder to buy and sell and may have a wide spread. (This generalization is not always true. There are some tiny illiquid companies mouldering on the main market too.) Many private investors like AIM companies, some shun them.

The newspaper also gives details of shares traded on three other markets, **OFEX, EASDAQ** and **EURO.NM**. OFEX is an unregulated trading facility, operated by J. P. Jenkins, for dealing in the shares of some unquoted companies. Many are tiddlers, but there are a few substantial companies, such as Weetabix.

EASDAQ and EURO.NM are battling it out to become Europe's answer to the US Nasdaq market, which specializes in innovative

72

companies, many from the technology field, and many quite large companies. Both markets are aimed at professional investors. Information on all three appears under the heading Other Markets.

TOP TIPS

New issues

Novice investors love new issues – shares offered for sale when a company launches itself on to the stock market. Yet all the statistics suggest that, on average, new issues do worse than the market as a whole. Avoid them, unless you are very certain of your reasons for buying them. The warning applies to new unit and investment trusts as well as new issues of company shares.

There are plenty of good reasons why newcomers are likely to be a bad bargain. First, issues tend to come in waves near the top of a bull market. So you are likely to be buying into the stock market at a bad time. Second, many companies arrive with the best of their growth behind them, or when stock market expectations for their kind of business are unrealistically high.

Benjamin Graham, the US investment guru, summed it up neatly. 'Most new issues are sold under "favourable" market conditions – which means favourable for the seller and, consequently, less favourable for the buyer.' If conditions are not favourable, the sellers can simply wait until they are: witness the way major issues get pulled if the market sags.

Of course there are some exceptions to this generalization. Shares in many of the privatizations did remarkably well for several years after their launch. But this was partly because the government priced them cheaply (it was scared of failing to get them away), partly because there was lots of scope for making the privatized companies leaner and meaner. Investment and unit trust launches depend on successful marketing, and often follow fashion at just the wrong time. 'Marketing and investment opportunities have an inverse relationship,' commented one investment trust analyst. The best time to invest in a market is before it goes up; the best time to market a fund to the public is after it has gone up.

With new issues, it pays to be suspicious, if not paranoid. As Graham put it: 'New issues have a special salesmanship behind them which calls for a special degree of sales resistance.'

Highs and lows: can you time the market?

Is it worth trying to time your investment in the stock market? Enough people seem to think so. At the start of each year, analysts reveal their targets for the FTSE 100 index or the Dow Jones Industrial Average and pundits pontificate on whether it is a good or bad time to enter the market

Whether all this analysis is worth it is another matter. End-year forecasts for indices have a remarkable tendency to be close to the current level plus 10 per cent (the long-term average annual gain). And surveys of investment advisers show that their bearishness or bullishness tends to be an excellent contrariant indicator; when everyone is bullish, there are no new buyers left.

One school of thought holds to the view that it is virtually impossible to pick the top and the bottom of the market. All investors achieve by trying to do this is incur dealing costs. The best strategy is to buy and hold, certain that equities will outperform in the long term.

Statistics can certainly be found to back this assertion. According to the equity–gilt study from Barclays Capital, equities have outperformed cash in 97 per cent of all ten-year periods since the First World War and gilts in 96 per cent of such periods.

But figures can prove so many things. It certainly would have helped investors to sell equities at the end of 1972 and avoid the 70.5 per cent drop in equity prices that followed over the next two years. And investors who 'bought and held' US equities at the peak in 1929 had to wait twenty-five years before they got their nominal capital back.

Bubbles also occur from time to time, when investors pay silly prices for shares, and there are times when shares are ridiculously cheap. But while it is easy to spot such occasions in retrospect – the summer of 1987, say, or early 1975 – is there a way of being wise at the right moment?

One obvious method is to look at the economic and valuation fundamentals that underpin the market. While there are no hard-and-fast rules, bull markets tend to be associated with at least some of the following: falling interest rates; easy credit conditions; steady or rapid economic growth; rising corporate profits; moderate or low inflation, and political stability.

Bear markets, in contrast, tend to be linked with rising interest rates; tighter credit; recession; falling corporate profits; rapid inflation, and political crisis. The first four factors were clearly associated with the bear market of 1929–32; the downturn of 1974–5 had just about the lot.

There tends to be more of a debate on whether the valuation measures themselves (such as price/earnings ratios and dividend yields) can be taken as an indicator that prices are about to fall. Acceptable valuation levels have changed over time: until the 1950s, it was quite common for equities to yield more than bonds; in the 1970s and 1980s, high inflation meant that investors regularly required double the yield from bonds that they expected from shares.

The US dividend yield dropped to an all-time low quite early in the 1990s bull market but this did not stop share prices from marching ahead. One reason seemed to be US taxation, which makes dividends less attractive to investors and encourages the use of share buy-backs as a means for companies to return cash.

Similarly, high price/earnings ratios in the 1990s were justified by low inflation. The argument was that, with low inflation, economies would be more stable, avoiding the boom-and-bust cycles of the past. That should make corporate earnings more predictable, giving investors the confidence to pay a higher multiple for such earnings.

Some old-timers were sceptical of such arguments, saying that it has been quite common in the past for investors to argue that it was 'different this time' at the top of the market.

Sure enough, when the dividend yield on the FTSE All-Share index dropped to its lowest level since the First World War early in 1998, most people dismissed the moment as irrelevant; the market fell soon after, though it has since recovered ground.

The study of fundamentals is far from an exact science but it may help tilt the odds slightly in your favour. Figures from M&G, the fund

KNIT YOUR OWN COPPOCK INDICATOR

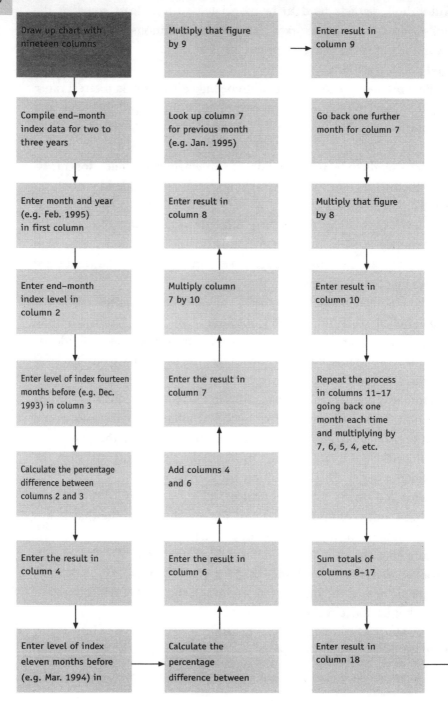

Draw up chart with nineteen columns

↓

Compile end–month index data for two to three years

↓

Enter month and year (e.g. Feb. 1995) in first column

↓

Enter end–month index level in column 2

↓

Enter level of index fourteen months before (e.g. Dec. 1993) in column 3

↓

Calculate the percentage difference between columns 2 and 3

↓

Enter the result in column 4

↓

Enter level of index eleven months before (e.g. Mar. 1994) in →

Multiply that figure by 9

↑

Look up column 7 for previous month (e.g. Jan. 1995)

↑

Enter result in column 8

↑

Multiply column 7 by 10

↑

Enter the result in column 7

↑

Add columns 4 and 6

↑

Enter the result in column 6

↑

Calculate the percentage difference between

→ Enter result in column 9

↓

Go back one further month for column 7

↓

Multiply that figure by 8

↓

Enter result in column 10

↓

Repeat the process in columns 11–17 going back one month each time and multiplying by 7, 6, 5, 4, etc.

↓

Sum totals of columns 8–17

↓

Enter result in column 18

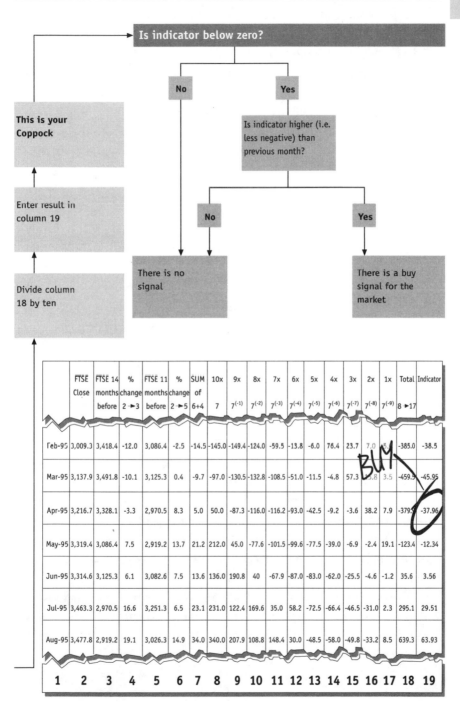

Is indicator below zero?

No → Yes

This is your Coppock

Is indicator higher (i.e. less negative) than previous month?

Enter result in column 19

No → Yes

Divide column 18 by ten

There is no signal

There is a buy signal for the market

	FTSE Close	FTSE 14 months before	% change 2 ►3	FTSE 11 months before	% change 2►5	SUM of 6+4	10x 7	9x $7^{(-1)}$	8x $7^{(-2)}$	7x $7^{(-3)}$	6x $7^{(-4)}$	5x $7^{(-5)}$	4x $7^{(-6)}$	3x $7^{(-7)}$	2x $7^{(-8)}$	1x $7^{(-9)}$	Total 8 ►17	Indicator 18 ►17
Feb-95	3,009.3	3,418.4	-12.0	3,086.4	-2.5	-14.5	-145.0	-149.4	-124.0	-59.5	-13.8	-6.0	76.4	23.7	7.0		-385.0	-38.5
Mar-95	3,137.9	3,491.8	-10.1	3,125.3	0.4	-9.7	-97.0	-130.5	-132.8	-108.5	-51.0	-11.5	-4.8	57.3	8.8	3.5	-459.5	-45.95
Apr-95	3,216.7	3,328.1	-3.3	2,970.5	8.3	5.0	50.0	-87.3	-116.0	-116.2	-93.0	-42.5	-9.2	-3.6	38.2	7.9	-379.5	-37.96
May-95	3,319.4	3,086.4	7.5	2,919.2	13.7	21.2	212.0	45.0	-77.6	-101.5	-99.6	-77.5	-39.0	-6.9	-2.4	19.1	-123.4	-12.34
Jun-95	3,314.6	3,125.3	6.1	3,082.6	7.5	13.6	136.0	190.8	40	-67.9	-87.0	-83.0	-62.0	-25.5	-4.6	-1.2	35.6	3.56
Jul-95	3,463.3	2,970.5	16.6	3,251.3	6.5	23.1	231.0	122.4	169.6	35.0	58.2	-72.5	-66.4	-46.5	-31.0	2.3	295.1	29.51
Aug-95	3,477.8	2,919.2	19.1	3,026.3	14.9	34.0	340.0	207.9	108.8	148.4	30.0	-48.5	-58.0	-49.8	-33.2	8.5	639.3	63.93

1   2   3   4   5   6   7   8   9   10   11   12   13   14   15   16   17   18   19

managers, show for example that there were thirty years between 1919 and 1989 when the dividend yield on the FTSE All-Share index was 5 per cent or more at the year end. In each case, there was a positive real (after inflation) rate of return on equities over the next five years.

The Coppock system outlined in the chart is a mechanical system for timing the market. The theory is that markets take time to recover from a setback, just as people take time to recover from grief. The man who devised the system, Edwin Coppock, asked the church how long it took people to recover from the loss of a loved one, and was told eleven to fourteen months; the system is thus based on eleven- and fourteen-month weighted averages.

Coppock only gives buy signals once every three years and so is not much use for an active trader; for the FTSE 100 index, the last signal was given at the end of April 1995, when Footsie was 3,216.7. It certainly worked that time. The index has never since ended a month below that level, and at its peak, in mid-July, had almost doubled.

It will be a while before a signal is activated again. After the recent correction, the indicator is headed down but is still positive; it needs to fall below zero and then turn up again before a signal can be given.

Another system developed by David Schwartz, the stock-market historian, also depends on buying the market after it has been depressed. In this case, it involves buying shares if the *FT* Non-Financials index is 10 per cent below its year-ago level. A qualification helps avoid long bear markets such as 1973–4: the index needs to be above its level six months previously.

Again this system does not throw up buy signals very often – fourteen times since 1950 – so it is only of occasional use.

Phased investment is one answer to the timing conundrum; putting £100 into an index fund each month avoids the problem of market tops and also benefits from the pound cost averaging principle (see below) – you buy more units when prices are low and fewer when prices are high.

However, it is far from a complete answer. It works for small savers but, for those with a large lump sum, phased investment may simply incur heavy costs and lead investors to be over-exposed to cash in a rising market.

So keeping an eye on the economic statistics and valuation measures should still be useful. As the investment guru Dooley Wilson advised in *Casablanca*: 'The fundamental things apply, as time goes by.'

VIEWPOINT

Long-term investor

Michael Hughes is director of asset allocation at Baring Asset Management and previously was a much respected strategist at Barclays de Zoete Wedd. After a long career in the City, he has a pretty philosophical approach towards market timing. 'You lose more money being out of the market than by being in it,' he says. 'For those who can afford to be long term, having a lifetime interest in the market is what is important. The question is whether, at cyclical peaks in the market, you should consume your dividends and, at lows, you should reinvest them.

Hughes also says that the development of derivatives since the early 1980s has made it much easier for market participants to adjust their levels of risk. That means that bear markets should be over much more quickly. 'The average bear market since the Second World War has lasted fourteen months and seen falls of 25 per cent. Well, [in mid 1998] falls of 25 per cent in less than fourteen weeks.'

But, over the medium term, he feels that the recent divergence between equities and bonds may reflect a more permanent shift. 'In the past, equities and bonds have moved together but shares have done better. In a low-inflation era, in which prices only rise to reflect quality improvement in products, it will in future pay investors to diversify their holdings into bonds.'

HOW THE FT CAN HELP

Valuation measures

Many of the valuation measures used to assess the UK stock market can be found on the back page of the second section of the *FT* Tuesday to Friday and in the first section on Saturday.

In the **market at a glance** section on the left-hand side, a table lists the closing values of the FTSE 100, 250, 350 and All-Share indices. It also shows the dividend yield on the All-Share, and readers could have spotted when the yield reached a post-First World War low in March 1998, a sign that equity prices were starting to get overvalued.

MARKET· AT A GLANCE

Indices and ratios

FTSE 100	4648.7	−101.7	FT 30	2806.8	−51.7
FTSE 250	4304.4	−38.3	FTSE Non-Fins p/e	18.60	18.97
FTSE 350	2233.5	−43.7	FTSE 100 Fut Dec	4699.0	−101.0
FTSE All-Share	2166.07	−43.21	10 yr Gilt yield	4.67	4.71
FTSE All-Share yield	3.62	3.55	Long gilt/equity yld ratio	1.27	1.31

Best performing sectors

1	Oil Exploration & Prod	+3.7
2	Tobacco	+2.0
3	Electronic & Elect Equip	+1.8

Worst performing sectors

1	Support Services	−6.2
2	Insurance	−4.8
3	Life Assurance	−4.6

The table also shows the yield on the benchmark ten-year gilt and the yield ratio – the relationship between long gilt and equity yields. For a long time, it was a good rule of thumb that shares were cheap when the yield ratio fell below 2, but in the autumn correction of 1998 that relationship broke down; the ratio reached 1.3 and equities were still falling.

Another useful statistic in the table is the price/earnings ratio on the *FT* **non-financial index** (used because banks often trade on a different basis from the rest of the market). Until 1999, the index was unable to sustain a historic p/e above 20 for very long, as proved to be the case in 1998.

In the bottom left-hand corner of the page is a much larger table, headed **FTSE actuaries share indices,** that gives a more detailed analysis of the market. Dividend yields and price/earnings ratios are given for all the leading indices including the SmallCap; it was possible to spot in early October 1998, for example, that the yield on the SmallCap (excluding investment trusts) index had risen above that on ten-year gilts.

The same part of the table also shows the cover level of the various indices – the higher the cover, the greater the scope for companies to raise their dividends.

Further down the table, the market is broken down into its various economic groups and industry sectors, with the key yield and price/ earnings ratios shown for each one. Valuation measures vary quite sharply between sectors, because of investors' differing perceptions of their growth prospects.

For example on 6 October, the paper, packaging and printing sector was on a dividend yield of nearly 6.9 per cent and a price/earnings ratio of 7.5 (the sector has been hit hard by the strong pound and fears of an economic slowdown); however the telecommunications sector was showing a yield of 2.3 per cent and a p/e ratio of 37.

For information on valuations of other stock markets, look on the **world stock markets** page (opposite the World Stock Market reports in the UK edition). That gives, where available, yields and p/e ratios for most of the major markets. On 6 October 1998, for example, Thailand was trading on a p/e of 46.8 while South Africa only commanded a multiple of 7.6; in yield terms, there was a big contrast between New Zealand (5.8 per cent) and Japan (1.1 per cent).

On the same page, there is a more detailed breakdown of ratios for the US stock market, which showed that, at the end of September 1998, the S&P 500 index was still yielding less than 1.5 per cent and trading on a price/earnings ratio of nearly 30, even after Wall Street's substantial third-quarter falls.

Pound cost averaging

Pound cost averaging is one of the bonuses that occasionally seem to favour the little people. Most of us start regular savings schemes (into unit trusts or ISAs) because we do not have sufficient capital to put a big lump sum into the market.

The averaging principle works in our favour because we invest a regular sum rather than buy a level number of units or shares. So we get more units when prices are low and fewer when prices are high.

Suppose you had put £100 a month into a FTSE 100 index fund on the fifteenth of each month from January to September 1998 (and that the price of one unit was one hundredth of the level of the index). The respective index levels were 5,165.8, 5,582.3, 5,782.3 6,074.1, 5,917.8, 5,715.7 6,151.5, 5,455.0 and 5,281.7 (quite a range).

In January, you would have got 1.936 units for your £100 (£100 divided by £51.658). But the following month, with the market higher, you would have only got 1.791 units, and in July at the peak of the market, a mere 1.626 units. By the end, you would have 15.894 units worth £839.47 (15.894 × £52.817, the price of a unit in September).

That would have been a loss on your original investment of 6.8 per cent (caused by the sharp fall in the last two months). But you would have been better off than if you had put all your money in at the market peak in July (which would have prompted a 14.1 per cent loss).

And, had you bought a regular number of units each month, say two, your loss would have been 7.0 per cent – £950.71 (18 × £52.817) compared with £1,022.53 (the cost of buying two units a month). The difference is small over a limited timescale, but should build up over time.

The averaging process works best when the markets are volatile, and there are two caveats. If the market rises steadily throughout the investment period, you would have done better to invest a big lump sum at the start; and if the market falls steadily over the investment period, you would obviously have done better not to invest at all.

Traditional share valuation measures

The stock market is a numbers game. Professional investors rely on several different yardsticks to assess the relative attractions of different shares. Here we explain what they do and how to interpret them

Whether you like to pore over individual company balance sheets, armed only with a pocket calculator, or rely on a computer program to 'screen' thousands of stocks for desirable characteristics, you will be relying on certain valuation yardsticks. Since markets began, investors have been searching for formulae that would enable them to cut through the tangled forests of figures and identify attractive value. Certain techniques have become tried and tested over the years, but in stock market investment nothing is simple, and all the valuation methods require careful interpretation.

● **Dividend yield.** The cash income – normally received twice a year in the form of an interim dividend and a, rather larger, final dividend – is the most basic foundation for share valuation. Over many decades, the overall market dividend yield in the UK has averaged between 4½ and 5 per cent before tax, although yields have generally been lower in overseas markets.

Dividend yields on individual stocks can be very variable, however. At present, yields varying between 10 and 0 per cent can be found within the constituents of the FTSE 100 Index (some of the hot telecommunications companies believe dividends are an irrelevance).

Two main questions need to be asked in assessing a dividend yield. First, how safe is it? If the next payment is cut, the apparently attractive yield of, say, 7 per cent may be largely an illusion. Usually the market's expectation of the next or prospective annual total dividend is more important for the share price than the amount actually paid in the past year. Stability of profits, and the cover – the ratio of available earnings to dividends – are also important factors here. Second, how rapidly is the dividend stream likely to grow? A fast growing dividend stream is clearly worth much more than a static one, and so growth stocks are worth buying on much lower initial yields than mature companies.

Professional analysts use dividend discount models to compute the impact of different growth assumptions. Due to the power of compound arithmetic, valuations can be very sensitive to the forecast of the growth rate and this explains why company shares can fall so sharply when they produce disappointing results or issue profit warnings.

Unfortunately the analysis of dividends has become more complex than it used to be. Tax changes introduced by Gordon Brown in his 1997 Budget, and fully enforced in April 1999, have reduced the appeal of ordinary dividends to pension funds and other investors (like PEP holders) who used to be able to reclaim income tax on dividends.

Companies are therefore much more interested than they used to be in finding alternative, more tax-efficient, ways of returning cash to shareholders. Share buy-backs are increasingly popular.

Analysts are concerned that it may be necessary to take buy-backs into account in valuing the dividend flows. Such considerations have already been important in the US in allowing dividend yields to fall a long way below historical levels – at the extreme, to only about 1.3 per cent on the S&P 500 Index in midsummer 1998. Even in the UK the market yield went as low as 1.23 per cent, indicating that shares had become very expensive – which indeed has subsequently turned out to be the case.

● **Price/earnings ratio.** There are many measures of profit, but a particular definition is earnings – the profits, after tax and any other charges, that are attributable to ordinary shareholders. Earnings are reported by companies on a per share basis, and that can be translated by analysts into an earnings yield, to parallel the dividend yield. Commonly, however, the ratio is presented the other way up, as the price earnings ratio: thus, a 5 per cent earnings yield represents a p/e ratio of 20.

Recently the market average historic p/e ratio in the UK has been about 18, which, in spite of the market's setback, remains above average by the standards of a normal historical range between 10 and 22. (This is not counting the 1970s, when it was much lower.) The higher the ratio, the more optimistic investors must be about growth in order to pay the market price. Thus growth stocks are on high p/es. Stocks on low p/es may represent bargains, but more likely they are facing troubled times. The challenge for the investor, of course, is to find companies that have better prospects than the market is pricing in. Again, the prospective p/e is more important than the historic one.

Earnings suffer from fundamental measurement problems because they depend on subjective judgements made by companies and their auditors. In bull markets, standards often deteriorate as companies bend the rules to meet the over-ambitious expectations of investors. At the end of the 1980s there was a series of accounting scandals in the UK, and recently the Securities and Exchange Commission in the US has complained of a serious decline in the quality of corporate reporting.

● **Net asset value.** Company balance sheets display a figure for the book value of shareholders' funds, which can be expressed as net worth per share. This used to be a very popular way of assessing value, and a related concept (the price to book ratio) is still used by quantitative analysts (the ones who use computers). But there is an old investment saying that 'assets are only worth what they can earn'. Asset analysis is most useful when companies possess unexploited assets that could be sold or put to other uses – office blocks, say, or stakes in other companies. Inflexible assets such as machinery or oil wells may need to be analysed more cautiously.

The decline of manufacturing industry has highlighted the importance of intangible assets to today's companies – brand names, software, royalty rights and the skills of the workforce. Because it is so hard to value these satisfactorily in the balance sheet the use of asset value analysis has declined in importance.

There have been parallel difficulties with a similar, but slightly more sophisticated, yardstick invented by the American economist James Tobin – the Q ratio. This is the ratio of a company's market capitalization to the replacement cost of its assets. It is commonly aggregated across the market as a whole, and in the 1970s and early

HOW TO DO THE SUMS

Company information needed
Company name **J. Sainsbury**

- Share price **560p** (14 Oct. 1998)
- Net annual dividend per share (historic) **13.9p**
- Net annual dividend per share (forecast) **15.3p**
- Annual earnings per share (historic) **27.4p**
- Annual earnings per share (forecast) **29.0p**
- Annual earnings growth (av. last 4 yrs) **1.1 per cent**
- Annual earnings growth (av. last 2 yrs) **−1.9 per cent**
- Annual earnings growth (av. next 2 yrs) **7.7 per cent**
- Sales per share **776p**
- Net asset value per share **216p**
- Net borrowing **£1,091m**
- Shareholders' funds **£4,112m**

Measuring the balance sheet

Price to book
Share price ÷ net asset value per share
560 ÷ 216 = 2.6

Gearing (%)
Net borrowings ÷ shareholders' funds x 100
£1,091m ÷ £4,112m x 100 = 26.5 per cent

Measuring the profit and loss account

Dividend yield, per cent (historic)
Net annual dividend per share (historic) ÷ share price x 100
13.9 ÷ 560 x 100 = 2.48 per cent

Dividend yield, per cent (forecast)
Net annual dividend per share (forecast) ÷ share price x 100
15.3 ÷ 560 x 100 = 2.73 per cent

Dividend cover (historic)
Annual earnings per share (historic) ÷ net annual dividend per share (historic)
27.4 ÷ 13.9 = 1.97

Dividend cover (prospective)
Annual earnings per share (forecast) ÷ net annual dividend per share (forecast)
29.0 ÷ 15.3 = 1.9

Price/earnings ratio (historic)
Share price ÷ annual earnings per share (historic)
560 ÷27.4 = 20.4

Price/earnings ratio (prospective)
Share price ÷ annual earnings per share (forecast)
560 ÷ 29 = 19.3

Price/earnings growth factor (historic)
P/e ratio (historic) ÷ annual earnings growth (av. last 4 years)
20.4 ÷ 1.1 = 18.5

Price/earnings growth factor (prospective)
P/e ratio (prospective) ÷ annual earnings growth (av. last 2 and next 2 years)
19.3 ÷ 2.9 = 6.6

Price to sales
Share price ÷ sales per share
560 ÷ 776 = 0.72

Source: FT, Company REFS August 1998. Historic statistics for year to end February 1998

Note: all earnings figures and ratio derived from them are normalized (see below)

88

1980s Q was usually less than 1, suggesting that companies were quite cheap.

In the 1990s, stock markets in the US and Europe have become very expensive by this benchmark. But the already mentioned qualitative problems apply, and the bulls have argued that the markets are not so expensive if the true value of intangible assets is factored in.

A particular case where asset values are especially important is that of the investment trust sector. These closed-end investment funds are priced according to the market value of their underlying investments, and they normally trade at discounts, which investors study closely in order to assess cheapness and dearness.

● **Other value measures.** Some investors like to consider not just earnings but also cashflow. There are several versions of this including net cashflow, which is undistributed earnings plus depreciation. Cashflow can give a better idea of the financial strength of a company, especially one which is capital-intensive.

A concept that has become popular in the past few years is the price/earnings growth factor, or PEG. This is the p/e ratio divided by the annualized growth rate of earnings. A PEG of significantly less then 1 is regarded as attractive, so a share with a moderate p/e ratio of 15 would need a growth rate of close to 20 per cent a year to be a strong buy.

There is also the price to sales ratio – simply the ratio of the total value of the company's equity (that is, its market capitalization) to its sales. This might seem a confusing indicator, because profit margins can vary so much between different kinds of industry. But, in an influential book *What Works on Wall Street*, published in 1996, the American quantitative investor James P. O'Shaughnessy concluded that in the US context, at any rate, this was the most useful analytical measure of all, when judged over several decades.

Finally, a word about gearing, or, as the Americans call it, leverage. It can be defined as the ratio of net borrowing to shareholders' funds. It is not a measure of value in itself, but provides a warning signal if it climbs above, say, 50 per cent. Stable businesses, however, can use high gearing quite safely as a way of boosting the return on equity; cyclical or risky businesses must be much more prudent.

COMPANY EARNINGS

Too much choice

Many investors have a touching belief in company earnings. Accountants and analysts are far more sceptical. First, it is not possible to distil the performance of a complex organization, such as a company, into a single measurement. Second, earnings are the product of subjective judgements, and can be fiddled.

In the bad old days, managers used to have effective discretion to categorize an unusual profit as 'exception', which meant it was included along with all the other profits in the earnings calculation, but decide that an unusual loss was 'extraordinary', out of the reckoning.

Accountants and analysts have done their best to curb managers' scope for creativity. But the result is several earnings figures for each company.

Since the start of this decade, the accountants' rules have required companies to itemize abnormal items, but they also require them to include virtually every profit or loss in the earnings calculation, even if it is obviously a one-off. Result: earnings per share became more unpredictable and volatile.

However, the analysts' association, the Institute of Investment Management and Research, promptly introduced a set of standard adjustments to the accountants' earnings figures. The IIMR adjustments exclude all capital transactions (such as the profit from an asset sale) from earnings. But any trading item, such as a bad debt, stays in. IIMR earnings, also known as headline earnings, are used for statistics, such as the *FT*'s London share service.

In practice, individual analysts also make further common-sense adjustments to the IIMR figures. The resulting figures, known as 'normalized earnings', are often referred to by journalists. Hence discrepancies between p/e ratios in different parts of the *FT*.

Dividend yields

The *FT* reprints the dividend yields for individual companies, on the **London Share Service pages**, and for market indices in the table headed **FTSE Actuaries share indices**. The yields quoted in the paper are actual, net (after tax) payments made by companies. The FT used to quote gross (before tax) figures, but stopped this in April 1999 after changes to the tax regime meant most investors lost the right to claim a tax credit on dividend payments.

	£ Stlg Jun 23	Day's chge%	Actual yield%	Cover	P/E ratio	Xd adj. ytd	Total Return
FTSE Actuaries Share Indic							UK Series
Produced in conjunction with the Faculty and							
FTSE 100	6496.5	−0.9	2.16	1.59	28.75	81.15	2913.97
FTSE 250	5906.9	−0.3	2.65	1.82	20.69	88.48	2611.03
FTSE 250 ex Inv Co	70.7	−0.	2.75	1.87			
Packaging(10)	2056.72		5.20	2.00	9.59	56.69	981.04
Personal Care & Hse Prods(4)	2273.94		3.46	1.70	16.97	41.42	996.49
Pharmaceuticals(21)	10110.01		1.68	1.29	45.94	114.97	3681.74
Tobacco(3)	7447.90		4.04	1.05	23.48	212.89	2190.03
CYCLICAL SERVICES(220)	3896.34		2.26	1.96	22.56	42.91	2191.88
Distributors(22)	2385.06		3.89	1.63	15.75	47.20	978.13
General Retailers(40)	2259.16		2.77	1.73	20.93	38.26	1421.11

Market sectors

Think relative. That is one of the first lessons a novice investor has to learn. Professional investors weigh up a share's attractions by comparing it with others in similar businesses.

It is easy to assume that you have found a bargain when you come across a share where the p/e ratio is substantially less than the market average. Take the leisure sector. (We are using the figures published in the 10 October 1998 newspaper.) If you run your eye down the London share service, you can find substantial companies such as Granada and Ladbroke with historic p/e ratios of 14 and 13 respectively, compared with a historic ratio of around 18 on the FTSE All-Share index. But that does not necessarily mean that either share is cheap.

Turn to the FTSE Actuaries share indices table and you will discover that the average p/e ratio for the leisure sector is just under 13. In this context both Granada and Ladbroke look a touch pricey. Analysts are gloomy about prospects for leisure and hotel companies.

Sector ratings vary a lot. Look higher up the table of indices and you can find pharmaceuticals with a p/e ratio of 38 and a gross yield of just over 2. Telecommunications is on 39; food retailers on a more mundane 18.

This disparity partly reflects the fact that investors expect much faster growth from businesses such as Glaxo and Vodafone than they do from J. Sainsbury and Tesco. But it also reflects the fact that they care more about p/e ratios in some sectors than others.

Shares in the same sector tend to move together, as analysts blow hot and cold on the sector. And the individual shares jostle for position as views of their relative attractions change. The private investor ignores sector relativities in large companies at his peril, for professionals dominate the market. Smaller companies are more often assessed in their own right.

Are you a tortoise or a hare?
Depending partly on your temperament, you are either a value investor or a growth investor. Value investors will buy only when they are sure of a profit. Growth investors are looking for the next big star on the horizon

Most good investment ideas are born in the United States. Value investment and growth investment are no exception. The principles of value investment were set down by Benjamin Graham, the father of investment analysis, in his classic textbook, *The Intelligent Investor*. Less well known is T. Rowe Price, another American fund manager, who invented growth stock investment.

The two schools are seen as opposites, partly because they use different criteria in selecting shares, but also because they appeal to different kinds of people. Value investors are painstaking, cautious and very reluctant to take risks. They only buy shares when the sums suggest that they cannot lose money by doing so. And they are happy to buy shares in a boring business or an unsuccessful company if they are convinced they are cheap and that the price will rise to remedy this. They are the kind of people who go into a hotel and check out the fire escape rather than the bar.

Growth investors are far more fun. They are enthusiasts and romantics: the kind of people who can say: 'This share is cheap at any price,' and almost mean it. They are looking for tomorrow's winners: wonderful little businesses that will beat the market year in and year out, and end up as Microsoft before you can blink. They aim to catch their companies young.

Value investors are checking out what is in the safe today; growth investors are gazing through rose-tinted glasses at what might be there tomorrow.

But those are the extremes. Graham and Price started with very different philosophies. But both were realists and modified their theories substantially before they died. Price's theories had become highly fashionable by the end of the 1960s and every fund manager was a growth investor – except Price. He declared that growth stocks had become too expensive; his followers carried on buying them until the 1974 bear market, when many of the most popular growth stocks lost over 80 per cent of their value.

Today Graham's best known disciple, Warren Buffett, has further modified his master's strategy. Whereas Graham relied almost entirely on quantitative criteria (sums). Buffett looks first at the quality of the underlying business. Only when he is satisfied with the business – and it takes a lot to satisfy Buffett – does he start doing sums. Then he is just as demanding as Graham, but his criteria are more forward-looking. Similarly, modern growth investors, such as Jim Slater, use many quantitative sieves when searching for growth stocks.

What is the difference between a modern value investor and a modern growth investor? Not a lot in some cases. Indeed, Buffett pooh-poohs the difference between the two schools. He argues that growth is simply the calculation used to determine value.

● **Classic value investment.** Graham recommended two types of investment systems. His first, intended for ordinary ignorant investors, was to buy a portfolio of undervalued blue chips, and hang on to them: he called this 'defensive' investment.

His alternative was 'aggressive' or 'enterprising' investment. And the only private investors who should attempt an enterprising strategy were those who knew enough about investment analysis to have the right to treat their portfolio as a business. For them, he set out a number of criteria for picking shares.

● **Bargain issues.** Graham was looking for companies where a fire sale of all the company's assets tomorrow would infallibly give today's investor more than his money back. His definition of a 'bargain issue' was a company where the current share price was less than the current net asset value per share. (In other words, you could forget about assets, such as buildings and machinery, that might be hard to sell. If you took the company's current assets such as stocks, cash and investments and knocked off its debts, would the resulting figure per share still be at least 50 per cent higher than the share price?) That one-third undervaluation was the stockpicker's safety margin, a concept dear to the heart of all value investors. The snag with this criterion is that it is usually impossible today to find any companies which satisfy it. Modern attempts to pick portfolios of bargain shares always use a less rigorous asset criterion.

● **Other Graham criteria.** Later in his life, Graham developed other criteria for selecting cheap shares and suggested investors should use at least two of the screens in combination. Three favourites, which remain in popular use today, are a low p/e ratio, a high dividend yield and low gearing.

The low p/e ratio ensures that the share price is low in relation to what the company has earned, or is expected to earn, for its shareholders. The high dividend yield ensures that the share price is low in relation to the income shareholders have received, or are expected to receive, from the company. And low balance sheet gearing (the ratio of debt to shareholders' funds) rules out companies with an intrinsically risky financial structure.

● **Additional value yardsticks.** Today's analysts sometimes vary the classic yardsticks. They may for example use price/sales ratios or price/cashflow ratios.

The object of the exercise in all cases is to buy shares when they are so cheap that they are unlikely to fall, even if something nasty happens. But it is equally important to know when to sell.

● **When to sell.** Graham's basic rule is to sell when the share has exhausted its safety margin. The investor hopes this will occur because the share price has risen. At worst, it will mean that the situation has deteriorated and the safety margin been whittled away, with no actual loss.

Classic value investing is a ruthless business. You buy shares because they are cheap, and sell them once they cease to be cheap. The business behind the share price is pretty irrelevant.

● **Modern value investment.** Warren Buffett acknowledges his debt to

Value vs Growth

96

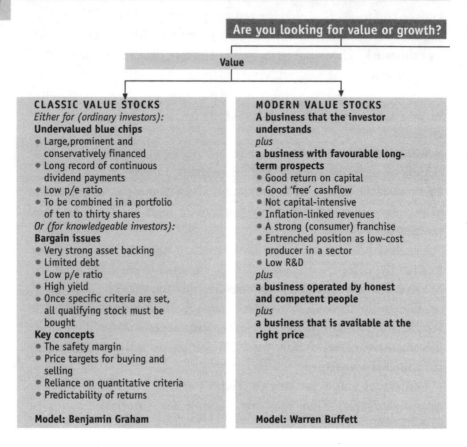

Graham, and subscribes to the basic theory that it is only worth buying shares where the numbers stack up and there is a safety margin. But Buffett famously will only buy good businesses with good management and good long-term prospects. What is more, he will only buy businesses he can understand. For only in these cases can he be confident that his expectations will be well founded. Like Graham, he demands certainty and aims to eliminate risk. His best known criteria are set out in the chart.

Buffett has always been a bit coy about what sums he does. One outside analyst, Robert Hagstrom, suggests that he uses a version of

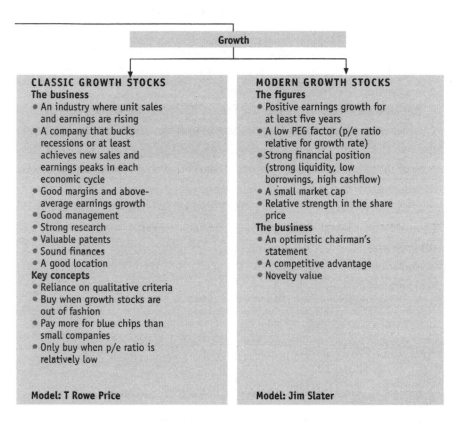

```
                            Growth
        ┌─────────────────────┴─────────────────────┐
        ▼                                            ▼
CLASSIC GROWTH STOCKS                    MODERN GROWTH STOCKS
The business                             The figures
 • An industry where unit sales           • Positive earnings growth for
   and earnings are rising                  at least five years
 • A company that bucks                    • A low PEG factor (p/e ratio
   recessions or at least                    relative for growth rate)
   achieves new sales and                  • Strong financial position
   earnings peaks in each                    (strong liquidity, low
   economic cycle                            borrowings, high cashflow)
 • Good margins and above-                 • A small market cap
   average earnings growth                 • Relative strength in the share
 • Good management                           price
 • Strong research                       The business
 • Valuable patents                        • An optimistic chairman's
 • Sound finances                            statement
 • A good location                         • A competitive advantage
Key concepts                               • Novelty value
 • Reliance on qualitative criteria
 • Buy when growth stocks are
   out of fashion
 • Pay more for blue chips than
   small companies
 • Only buy when p/e ratio is
   relatively low

Model: T Rowe Price                      Model: Jim Slater
```

discounted cashflow analysis. In other words, he works out what he expects the company to earn in future, and value for the shares (see page 54). Somewhat surprisingly, the discount rate he uses for his sums is less cautious than that used by most equity analysts. He chooses the risk-free rate of return – without any loading for the additional equity risk. But that is why he will only buy businesses he can understand. For only then can he be confident that his predictions are accurate. His safety margin lies in the fact that he will only buy the shares if he can get them at well below what he considers their present value to be.

Once he has tracked down one of these cheap paragons, Buffett is willing to hold it virtually for ever.

● **Growth shares.** We shall be looking at growth investment in detail on page 103. The chart on page 96 lists some of the main stockpicking criteria set out by T. Rowe Price and Jim Slater.

● **Which system works best?** Value stocks traditionally do best when the market as a whole has been low but is set to recover; growth stocks do best when the bull market is running hard.

But beware – in many cases the faster they rise, the harder they fall.

Mike Lenhoff at broker Capel-Cure Myers has analysed the results of the two different approaches when applied to large companies over the period 1972–95. Value beat growth overall, but there were long periods in which growth did best.

He argues that, eventually, growth stocks fail to fulfil their original promise and disappoint investors. Conversely, value stocks tend to be under-appreciated, and sooner or later they surprise the market favourably. Fallen angels become the seeds for tomorrow's value stocks, and vice versa.

MASTERCLASS

Buffett basics

Why does Warren Buffett get quoted so often? Partly because he is an out-standingly successful investor, who has built Berkshire Hathaway up into a company twice the size of General Motors. Partly because he is adept at producing homespun soundbites.

'I have seen no trend towards value investing in the thirty-five years I've practised it. There seems to be some perverse human characteristic that likes to make easy things difficult.'

'Berkshire buys, when the lemmings are heading the other way.'

'If the business does well, the stock eventually follows.'

'Pension fund managers continue to make decisions with their eyes firmly fixed in the rear-view mirror.

'Risk comes from not knowing what you are doing.'

'Forecasts usually tell us more of the forecaster than of the future.'

'My idea of a group decision is to look in the mirror.'

'Investment must be rational; if you can't understand it, don't do it.'

'I want to be able to explain my mistakes. This means I only do things I completely understand.'

'Read Ben Graham and Phil Fisher, read annual reports but don't do equations with Greek letters in them.'

'An investor cannot earn superior profits from stocks simply by committing to a specific category or style. He can earn them only by carefully evaluating facts and continuously exercising discipline.'

Most of these quotations were taken from Janet Lowe's collection, Warren Buffett Speaks. *Buffett's legendary letters to shareholders in Berkshire's annual reports can be obtained for a token sum from the company in Omaha, Nebraska.*

HOW THE FT CAN HELP

Company information

Company information is the lifeblood of all stockpicking systems. The main place to find it in the *Financial Times* is the second section of the Monday to Friday paper, which is devoted to **companies and markets.** The front page includes the most interesting news stories of the day, usually a mix of UK and international news. But it also includes an index that allows you to see at a glance whether there is an article about a particular company, and also shows you where to find the statistical tables. It is worth checking out the back page market reports too in case they mention a company you are interested in.

Detailed reports of UK company announcements and news come immediately after the front page. The daily results table provides a snapshot of the day's crop. If it is a very small company with run-of-the-mill results, this may be the only mention it gets. Our example shows the table published on 7 October 1998. Take Alexandra, which supplies overalls and other working clothes. In the first half year, its turnover is slightly down, which is not encouraging, but profits and earnings are both well up, and the dividend is well covered by earnings. The footnotes refer to an exceptional charge, which suggests that the company had some problems a year or so back.

Weekday

RESULTS					
	Turnover (£m)	Pre-tax profit (£m)		EPS (p)	Current payment (
Alexandra .... 28 wks to Aug 15★	35.3 (36)	3.47	(2.33♠)	7 (4.4)	2.5
Berry Birch & Noble.... 6 mths to July 31	4.41 (4.12)	0.421♠	(0.177)	6.1 (1.3)	1
Carbo .... 6 mths to July 31	41.9 (45.3)	0.22L♠	(0.701▼)	0.43L (0.43)	0.5

Weekend Money

■ Results due next week						■ Last v
			Dividend (p)*			
Company	Sector	Anncmnt due	Last year Interim	This year total	Last year Interim	Company
FINAL DIVIDENDS						Alpha Airports
Bridport	Eng	Wednesday	1.8	4.55	-	Andrews Sykes
BWI	Eng	Thursday	3	5	-	Ashley (Laura)
Galliford	Cnst	Thursday	0.5	1.05		Austin Reed

Turn to the **London share service** on the same day and you would find Alexandra nestling in the Household Goods and Textiles sector, with a gross dividend yield of over 10 per cent and a p/e ratio of less than 6. It is obviously not considered a high flying, growth company, and it has some of the characteristics of a bargain share. But you need a lot more information about it before you can begin to make a realistic judgement.

Fortunately, the ♣ mark against the company's name in the share price pages shows that it belongs to the **FT free annual reports club**. This allows you to phone for a copy of the latest annual and interim reports. These should help you work out some of the other standard investment yardsticks. But do not get too excited. Alexandra's recent record has been uninspiring. And, although there have been some management changes, a workwear company could have a tough time over the next few years if recession does bite.

Results or announcements from larger companies, or more dramatic announcements, get more detailed coverage in the *FT*. News stories normally include comments from the management, the share price reaction and a forecast from a broker who follows the company. If it is a very large company, or a very interesting announcement, there may be additional comment in the Lex column on the back page of Section

One. Alternatively, there is sometimes a comment attached to the news report in the companies section.

Anyone who missed the relevant paper during the week, can catch up in the Weekend paper. Weekend Money carries a summary of all the **interim and preliminary annual results** announced in the previous week. It also includes a table showing some of the results due over the forthcoming week. Unfortunately the latter is not comprehensive as companies are no longer obliged to notify the Stock Exchange of imminent results.

TOP TIP

Directors' dealings

Directors' share dealings have always been a popular investment indic-ator. If you see the board selling shares hand over fist, it is tempting to follow their example. Similarly, if you see them buying, it is reasonable to argue that they must be in the best position to know whether the shares are cheap. But be careful. Some directors' share dealings are significant, but a lot are not.

The last time we checked out the success rate of the deals highlighted in Weekend Money's table of directors' dealings, the results were as fol-lows. Overall, the shares picked out as possible buys did slightly better than the market; those picked out as possible sells did slightly worse.

But there were only a handful of really useful signals in more than a year. So how do you tell which they are?

The Inside Track, the firm which supplies the *FT* with its table of directors' dealings, has some basic rules:

● Many directors have substantial holdings in the companies they are directors of. (This is a normally a good sign: many top investors will only buy if the management has a stake in the action.) Look at any new share purchase in the light of the existing holding. If the purchase increases the holding by around 10 per cent, it is worth a second glance.

● Pay attention whenever several directors deal at the same time. But do remember that new directors often buy token stakes – nothing significant about that.

● Look at the director's earlier purchases and sales. A series of large sales is not offset by a small subsequent purchase, or vice versa.

● Deals a couple of months before the company's results can be significant, for directors are not supposed to deal in the run-up to results. This is their last chance.

● Deals by the chief executive or finance director usually matter most; those by non-execs usually least.

● If a particular director has a notably good track record in timing his sales and purchases profitably, he may be worth following.

● But if a single director is the only buyer on the scene, be careful. He may be mounting a one-man campaign to prop up the price.

Finding the next Microsoft

Most investors long to find a share that will bring them untold wealth.
But, by their very nature, high-growth stocks are not easy to spot. And,
once a growth stock falters, its price can fall as fast as it rose

Finding the wonder growth stocks ranks somewhere up there with selecting eight draws on the football pools and winning the National Lottery. It is a single development that could make you very rich.

Peter Lynch, the US fund manager who was in charge of the Fidelity Magellan fund for much of its phenomenal growth period, talks of finding the 'tenbagger', the stock that increases your wealth tenfold.

And the rewards can be even greater. Had you bought shares in Glaxo, the UK drugs company, in 1980, your money would have risen in value thirty-three times by the peak of the 1987 bull market. And the likes of Microsoft have made many employee shareholders millionaires.

So how do you go about finding the right growth stock? The obvious answer is that, if it were easy, we would all be doing it. For every Glaxo or Microsoft, there are a dozen drug or technology companies that have crashed in flames or simply failed to beat the market.

But 'growth' in this sense needs to be carefully defined. The ideal growth stock needs already to have demonstrated that it can deliver profits (and normally sales) growth well above the general level of the market. And it needs to have the prospect of delivering that growth for several years into the future.

If a stock has those characteristics, growth investors will tend to pay a high price for it. They will not be too concerned about paying a high price/earnings ratio (although a useful valuation mechanism called the PEG is examined below) or receiving a low dividend yield. If the company is growing strongly, it will be reinvesting its earnings in the business, and investors will be more concerned with capital gains than income.

The reason is that the laws of compound interest work on a growth stock's side.

Take two shares. One pays a 10p dividend but has earnings that are growing at 25 per cent a year. The other pays a 30p dividend, but its earnings are growing at only 5 per cent, the market average. In both cases, assume the payout ratio is constant.

The traditional method for valuing shares is to add up the future dividend payments and discount them to find a value. The discount rate is calculated by taking a risk-free return (the yield on gilts) and adding a risk premium to account for the uncertainties involved in holding equities. In this case, let us assume a gilt yield of 5 per cent and a risk premium of 4, making a discount rate of 9 per cent.

Because no company can grow at an above-market rate for ever (see below), the convention is to assume a limited period of rapid growth and then to assess what the company will be worth at that point – the 'terminal value' – calculated with regard to the predicted market yardsticks at the time. In this case, let us make it ten years and assume the market yield then will be 4 per cent.

The sum itself is complicated, though there are spreadsheets and tables that can do it for you. But for these shares the net present value of the high-growth shares comes out at around £11.83, while the low-growth shares are worth just £7.71. That is why the high-growth shares are still popular even though they only offer a yield of 0.8 per cent (10p divided by £11.83 × 100), and why the low-growth shares have to offer a much higher yield, 3.9 per cent (25p divided by £7.71 × 100). They are the bread today, while the high-growth shares are the jam tomorrow.

So what kind of stocks can offer such remarkable growth rates? They tend to fall into a few categories:

● **The new industry.** The company is involved in a sector which is just at the start of a long-term growth period that promises to turn what is currently a minority product into something that is owned by the bulk of the population. An obvious example at the moment is mobile phones; in the past, one might have chosen microwave-oven manufacturers or personal-computer makers. The risk here is that lots of businesses try to muscle in on the industry and, while sales grow for the sector, individual corporate profits are squeezed by the competition.

Rapid growth can also occur in businesses that perfect a successful formula in one region and then extend it to other areas in the country. This works particularly well in the US, which is a huge and fairly homogenous market; WalMart has been one of the classic growth stocks of the past twenty years, having extended its 'low price, big product range' formula from Arkansas to the rest of the country. It is normally more difficult, but not impossible, to extend formulas to international markets.

• **The 'better mousetrap' company.** This is a business that has a wonder product, possessed by none of its rivals, that customers are eager to snap up. A good recent example has been Raisio, the Finnish company that produces Benecol, the cholesterol-reducing margarine. The danger is that competitors rush in to produce close substitutes for the product and the initial marketing advantage fades away. This has been particularly the case for the technology industry.

But companies can avoid this danger if there are barriers to entry in their industry. A classic example is the pharmaceutical sector, where companies are given the protection of patent periods in which no one else can reproduce their product. Glaxo's growth in the 1980s owed much to just one drug, Zantac, the anti-ulcer treatment.

• **The franchise.** These are companies that have such a strong brand name or market position that they are likely to enjoy good growth rates for the foreseeable future. Such stocks are strongly favoured by Warren Buffett, the highly successful US investor.

Companies such as Coca-Cola, Intel and Microsoft dominate their sectors, and it would take a potential rival many years and billions of dollars to try to challenge them. In the case of consumer-goods companies like Coca-Cola, they have the opportunity of breaking into new areas of the world such as China.

The danger with this type of stock is that it is such an obvious selection that everyone jumps on the bandwagon and the price moves up to ridiculous levels. In the early 1970s, there was a group of stocks called the 'Nifty Fifty', of which it was believed that it did not matter what

FINDING A GROWTH STOCK

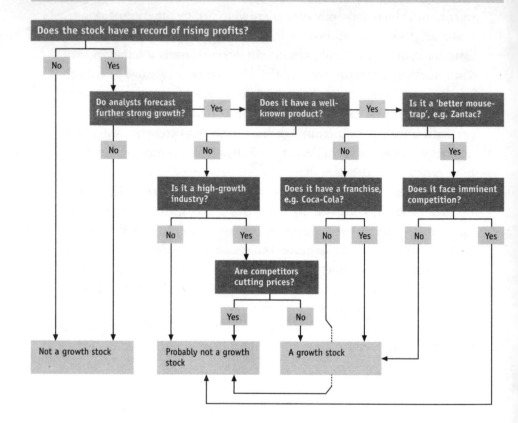

price you paid for them, because they would always deliver a sufficient level of growth to justify the investment. Those who bought the story and the stocks were savagely disappointed in the bear market of 1973–4.

Indeed, with all types of growth stocks, the penalties for disappointment are substantial. This is because the market tends to award a high rating to companies with high growth expectations. When the earnings fail to match expectations, investors take another look at the rating as well as the earnings forecasts.

Take a company whose earnings are expected to grow by 25 per cent next year (from 20p to 25p) and whose shares have a prospective earnings multiple (another term for p/e ratio) of 25, making them 625p. The company issues a warning that growth will only be 15 per cent.

That is not a bad growth rate by normal standards but the result is devastating for the share price. Earnings will now grow only to 23p and the multiple might fall to 15, taking the shares down to 345p, a fall of 45 per cent.

Which brings us back to the laws of compound interest again. Above-average growth for all growth companies will eventually peter out.

Remember the parable of the Shah of Persia and the inventor of chess, who asked as his reward one grain of wheat for the first square, two for the second, four for the third and so on. The request sounded reasonable but long before the sixty-fourth square, the Shah was required to provide more than the entire world wheat production.

The trick is to catch companies early in their growth rather than late. The good news is that during the early stage, there are lots of 'doubting Thomases' when it comes to the company's prospects and the rating is therefore more demanding; the bad news is that it is far more difficult to spot which companies are in a long-term uptrend and which have just enjoyed one or two bumper years.

It can also be tough to spot the top for growth stocks. One sign is when analysts start to mark down their forecasts for future years, although investors need to be pretty nimble because the market can respond very quickly to such shifts; another sign is when the stock starts to underperform the rest of the market. The latter factor can prove self-perpetuating as so-called 'momentum' investors (those who buy shares that are outperforming) bale out of the stock.

But usually the worst mistake with growth stocks is to get out too soon. All too often, portfolios are filled with so many duds that it takes the odd star stock to rescue the performance.

PROFILE

Buying for growth

Each fund manager has his or her own preferences when looking for a growth stock, and the difference between 'growth' and 'value' is less cut and dried than academic distinctions would suggest.

All investors are, at heart, looking for value stocks; it goes without saying that no one specifically seeks to buy shares which are overvalued.

Peter Chambers, director of active equities at Gartmore, says most investors look for stocks that can produce above-average earnings per share and sales growth stretching into the future.

'We think those stocks are very rare,' he says. 'Very few stocks can grow earnings faster than average for more than four years.'

Gartmore looks for stocks that can produce unexpected earnings growth that will beat the market over the next two to three years.

'We are ambivalent about whether those stocks are in the traditional growth category or merely bounding back from recession.'

Generating excess profit growth, says Chambers, is often about expanding margins or increasing asset turnover – that is growing sales without a big increase in working capital.

Chambers' team seeks out such companies by assessing industries, visiting the businesses concerned and compiling its own profits forecasts, which it compares with the market consensus. Obviously, it is looking for companies where the profit potential is as yet unrecognized by the market.

Valuations are then assessed using various multiples of cashflow and cross-checked with measures such as the price/earnings ratio and PEG (see below), or enterprise value to EBITDA (earnings before interest, tax, depreciation and amortization).

Price-earnings/growth factor

Judging whether a growth stock is cheap or expensive is a difficult task, with not much margin for error. A growth stock that disappoints will see its shares savaged.

One method of analysis is to calculate a PEG, or price-earnings/ growth factor. This compares the price/earnings ratio of a stock with the growth rate of its earnings per share.

If the p/e is less than the growth rate, all well and good. If it is around half the growth rate (according to Peter Lynch, the former head of the Fidelity Magellan fund) or 0.6 of the rate (according to Jim Slater), the shares may be highly attractive.

So a stock that is growing at 20 per cent a year but is trading on a price/earnings ratio of 12 may turn out to be a bargain.

In contrast, a stock that is trading on a rating twice its growth record may be too expensive. Beware, say, a company trading on a p/e of 40 but producing annual earnings growth of under 20 per cent.

Finding these figures can be a little cumbersome. The *Financial Times* publishes a price/earnings ratio for most stocks, and company comments, written at the time of the results, give estimates of the next year's earnings growth.

The Slater method uses four years of earnings for its calculations, of which two can be in the future (i.e. based on analysts' forecasts). That will require a handbook such as *Company REFS* or the *Estimate Directory* and possibly the company's annual report.

Slater adds a couple of sieves to weed out risky stocks. First, the company must have cashflow per share that exceeds earnings per share over the past year and as an average over the previous five years. This is designed to weed out companies that have been using 'creative accounting' to boost their profits.

The second test is to choose only those companies that have outperformed the market over the past month and year. All too often, the markets know there is 'something wrong' with a company and start to sell the shares well before analysts downgrade their forecasts or the companies themselves make a statement.

The main danger from this method lies in the reliance on analysts' forecasts. Analysts have a tendency to extrapolate from past trends and sometimes are unwilling to offend a company by making dramatic cuts in estimates. This can mean that forecasts are very slow to adjust to changes in trend.

Nor does the method do anything to cope with those companies, such as biotech groups that do not yet have any earnings at all but evidently have long-term growth potential.

In those cases, approaches such as 'price per pop' (based on the number of people in the potential market) or price to sales may do the trick. These yardsticks at least allow investors to compare the valuations of growth stocks in the same industry.

But for many companies, the PEG at least operates as a checking mechanism to ensure that investors are not getting so carried away by the growth prospects that they forget to worry about the price.

Portfolio size

There is no consensus on the ideal size of a private investor's stock portfolio.

It is generally agreed that a portfolio should not be so small that a disaster in one stock will irretrievably damage the investor's performance; or so large that it merely becomes an expensively run index fund. Remember also that the more stocks you own, the more time it takes to research them.

An old rule of thumb used to be that ten or twelve stocks was about the right level, although some people opted for twenty. But stock-picking exercises designed to exploit anomalies in the market have used much larger samples. Margaret Allen's Jim O'Shaughnessy, the US fund manager, has found that portfolios of, say, the fifty stocks with the lowest price-to-sales ratio have been shown to outperform the market.

The monetary size of the portfolio is obviously a key consideration. Dealing costs mean you would need to be reasonably affluent to build up a fifty-stock fund.

The benefits of diversification will only come through if you are truly diversified; having twelve stocks is no protection if they are all in the building materials sector, for example.

There is no harm in making a bet on a particular economic view, provided that you know what you are doing. A portfolio split between, say, chemicals, engineering, and paper and packaging is a gamble on a cyclical recovery, rather than a diversified basket. Another way of analysing your portfolio is to look at how volatile it is compared to the market. The correlation between a stock and the market is known as its beta; stocks with a beta of more than 1 go up faster when markets are rising and go down more quickly when they are falling (see page 39).

If you are very confident about the overall direction of the market, then you should look for a portfolio with a beta of more than one; if you are cautious about the overall market, but confident you can pick stocks, aim for a beta of less than one.

How to satisfy your investment wanderlust

Buying overseas stocks has become a lot easier following liberalization of markets across the world. But for the small investor there are some significant dangers that need to be considered first

The UK is a small island off the north-west coast of Europe with an economy that is a middle-ranker in world terms. It seems hard to imagine it can provide everything an equity investor needs.

But buying overseas-listed stocks remains, for private investors at least, a minority pursuit. A number of factors make it more difficult – increased costs, restricted information and currency risk. Nevertheless, for the well-off investor who already has a diversified portfolio of individual UK stocks, a selection of overseas holdings may be worth considering.

While the UK has its own technology sector, it does not have companies that dominate their industry sectors on the scale of Microsoft or Intel. There are no domestically quoted car manufacturers. And even in industries where the UK does have representatives such as mobile telephones, it may be from time to time that other global stocks in the sector look more attractive.

Buying overseas stocks has become a lot easier. UK foreign exchange controls were abolished in 1979 and markets have been liberalized all over the world to allow foreign investors to own stocks (although Malaysia recently moved in the opposite direction).

More information is now available (and, importantly, in English). 'There is a lot of information available on the internet,' says Paul Killik of Killik, the stockbrokers. 'Many companies have web sites that give all the relevant financial data.'

The *Financial Times* also covers the results and corporate developments relating to a host of leading companies from across the globe.

Before choosing an overseas stock, however, investors need to be clear about a number of factors.

First, a certain amount of international exposure can be achieved merely by investing in the UK market – around 50 per cent of the earnings of FTSE 100 companies come from overseas.

Second, if the main reason for your investment wanderlust is to gain exposure to another geographical location, you may need to be very well off. To build a properly diversified portfolio you need a minimum of ten stocks; add in the fact that dealing costs are higher for overseas stocks and this is clearly not an option for the small investor.

For any investor with just a few thousand pounds available, the best option is going to be a unit or investment trust specializing in a particular region. A fund will provide the necessary diversification at a much lower cost than private investors can achieve on their own.

It is also worth remembering the risks. In effect, most overseas stocks present the investor with two separate variables – the share price of the company concerned and the currency in which the share is denominated.

Most UK-based investors have their liabilities in sterling so it makes sense for them to have their assets in sterling too. Even if it had been possible to find an outstanding stock in south-east Asia or Russia over the past year, any capital gain would have been wiped out by the currency depreciation against the pound.

There are also differences in accounting and regulatory standards between countries, making it important to be extra careful when selecting individual shares. Good advice is essential.

Charges will also be greater when buying overseas stocks (see Top tip, page 121), reflecting the higher costs incurred by the broker, settlement charges imposed by overseas exchanges, the cost of converting currencies and so on.

'Value' plays might not always be as successful as in the UK. It might seem obvious that a poorly performing company is ripe for takeover, but in practice cross-holdings in the hands of friendly industrialists or political constraints make the group safe from predators. That said, one can invest in companies in the US and, increasingly, continental Europe with confidence that minority private investors will be given a fair crack of the whip.

The most likely area of interest is going to be blue-chip companies in the S&P 500 index or the FTSE Eurotop 300. Even if this is a restricted group, there is a lot of investment choice that is unavailable in the UK.

The US offers much fuller technology and biotechnology sectors than Europe, plus a host of global brand names such as Coca-Cola, Kodak and Gillette. While we await the flotation of Airbus, Boeing is the only aircraft manufacturer available to buy.

Believers in the prospects of the car industry can pick from a host of European stocks including BMW, Fiat and Volvo. Anyone hoping for a cyclical rebound in the chemicals industry has many more companies than just ICI to choose from, including Akzo, BASF and Hoechst.

Of course, because these blue-chip names are so well known, they can often command a premium rating and they tend to be the first choice for institutional, as well as for private, investors. In the 1995–8 bull market these shares tended to rise faster than the market as a whole. However, in recent months, some of these so-called 'New Nifty Fifty' have taken a battering as they tend to be the first stocks to be sold in a crisis.

So the private investor needs to be careful not to be one of the 'sucker buyers' – those lured into a stock at the top of the market just so the smart money can take its profits.

Over the longer term, the interest of private investors in all countries in overseas stocks seems likely to increase.

The creation of a single currency zone in Europe will mean that, for people in the 11 member countries of the euro, there will be no currency risk in investing in each other's stocks.

The UK will not be a member of the first wave of the euro, but many people expect it to join sometime before 2005. Even before then, the planned link between London and Frankfurt may prove the first step in the creation of a Europe-wide exchange in which a common set of stocks is traded using the same settlement system, making dealing easier and cheaper for all concerned.

In the very long run, there might even be a global electronic exchange

World markets

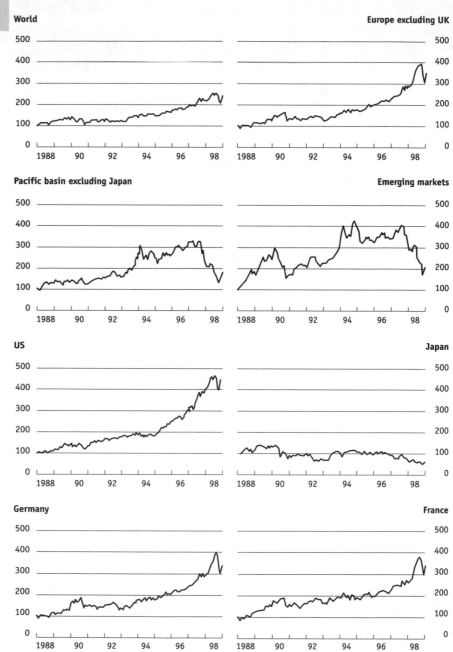

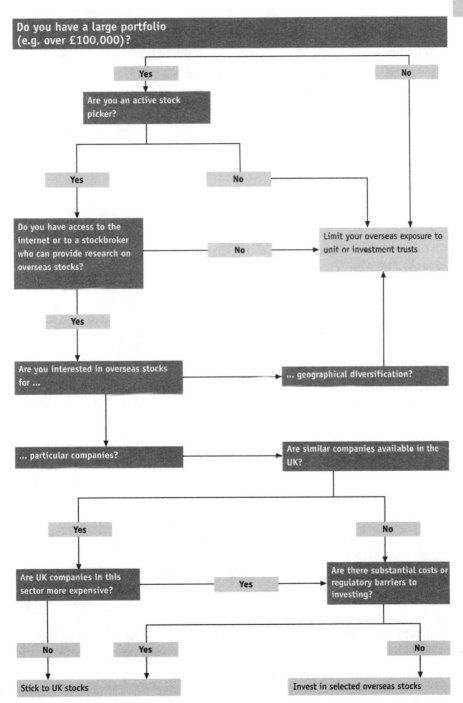

Do you have a large portfolio (e.g. over £100,000)?

Yes → Are you an active stock picker?

No → Limit your overseas exposure to unit or investment trusts

Are you an active stock picker?
- Yes → Do you have access to the internet or to a stockbroker who can provide research on overseas stocks?
- No → Limit your overseas exposure to unit or investment trusts

Do you have access to the internet or to a stockbroker who can provide research on overseas stocks?
- No → Limit your overseas exposure to unit or investment trusts
- Yes → Are you interested in overseas stocks for ...

Are you interested in overseas stocks for ...
- ... geographical diversification? → Limit your overseas exposure to unit or investment trusts
- ... particular companies? → Are similar companies available in the UK?

Are similar companies available in the UK?
- Yes → Are UK companies in this sector more expensive?
- No → Are there substantial costs or regulatory barriers to investing?

Are UK companies in this sector more expensive?
- No → Stick to UK stocks
- Yes → Are there substantial costs or regulatory barriers to investing?

Are there substantial costs or regulatory barriers to investing?
- Yes → Stick to UK stocks
- No → Invest in selected overseas stocks

with common listing and settlement rules; geographical barriers will disappear.

In fact, the battle may already be beginning. Nasdaq, the US electronic exchange, has recently mounted an advertising blitz in Europe and a European equivalent, Easdaq was launched in 1996. In the same year, four smaller European exchanges, Germany's Neuer Market, the Nouveau Marché in Paris and small-company exchanges in Amsterdam and Brussels joined together to form the Euro. NM.

The investor of tomorrow may need to be a man or woman of the world.

PROFILE

Stocks not countries

Anthony Bolton is a successful UK fund manager who has also produced an excellent long-term record running Fidelity's European unit trust in London.

He says the main difference between his European and UK funds is that the former has a larger proportion of big stocks – to meet the need for liquidity. When stockpicking on the continent, he looks for shares with a number of characteristics:

- **Industry anomalies.** In the past, Norwegian oil drilling companies have sold at a 50 per cent discount to US equivalents. Such discrepancies should eventually disappear.
- **Recovery situations.** Not straight cyclical plays such as chemicals, but companies where the business has gone wrong and is being put right. A good current example is Club Med.
- **Undervalued growth stocks.** Not the classic growth plays such as SAP, the German software company, but companies that may be little followed by analysts or have a complex story to tell.
- Businesses where there is a great likelihood of **corporate activity**, perhaps because there is a large holder of stock who seems likely, one day, to sell.
- **Asset discounts.** Some holding companies own large chunks of well-known companies but trade at a discount to the sum of their parts.

- **Controversial or risky stocks** in businesses that some investors shun, such as gambling or tobacco.

Bolton says the transparency of accounting has improved and that European companies are steadily becoming more shareholder-friendly, but it does vary from country to country, with southern Europe and Germany lagging behind. His geographical asset allocation arises from his individual stockpicks rather than being imposed in a 'top down' fashion.

HOW THE FT CAN HELP

Euro prices

The **euro prices page** was introduced in 1998 as an extra service to readers ahead of European monetary union in 1999.

The aim is to bring together on one page as much information as possible about the eurozone of eleven countries that have joined the first phase of the single currency process.

FTSE Actuaries Share Indices						European series
Produced in conjunction with the Faculty and Institute of Actuaries						
Jun 23	Euro Index	Day's %	change points	Yield gross %	xd adj ytd	Total retn (Euro) €
FTSE Eurotop 300	1328.82	−1.18	−15.89	1.91	17.16	1386.80
FTSE E300 Euroblnc	1360.81	−0.95	−13.06	1.82	18.12	1409.17
FTSE E300 Ex-Eurobloc	1307.88	−1.41	−18.67	2.00	16.45	1372.66
FTSE E300 Ex-UK	1343.52	−0.99	−13.44	1.75	17.92	1387.60
FTSE Eurotop 100	3070.72	−1.07	−33.24	1.86	40.49	1116.03
FTSE Eurobloc 100	1093.94	−0.91	−10.01	1.84	14.51	1125.76
FTSE EuroMid	1353.05	−0.89	−12.17	2.46	22.27	1426.47
FTSE EuroMid Eurobloc	1273.98	−0.60	−7.71	2.26	19.72	1321.73
FTSE EuroMid Ex-UK	1350.11	−0.71	−9.71	2.11	20.63	1396.92
FTSE Eurotop 300 Industry Sectors						
RESOURCES	1183.98	+0.15	+1.74	2.32	17.24	1258.23
Mining	1152.78	−3.94	−47.30	1.70	21.37	1206.09
Oil & Gas	1142.46	+0.47	+5.33	2.37	16.42	1188.77
BASIC INDUSTRIES	1245.24	−1.24	−15.65	2.53	25.05	1298.97
Chemicals	937.26	−0.95	−9.01	2.44	20.00	974.91
Construction & Bld Matls	1142.80	−1.93	−22.45	2.22	9.73	1163.13
Forestry & Paper	1184.70	−1.52	−18.24	2.26	38.68	1288.00

The article at the top of the page covers a topic of particular interest to the eurozone equity, debt or currency markets. The page also focuces on the FTSE Eurotop indices. These indices, set up by FTSE International (jointly owned by the *Financial Times* and the Stock Exchange), cover the leading stocks in Europe.

The creation of the eurozone has eliminated currency risk for investors in member countries who have started looking at the continent as a whole rather than at individual countries. Investors are beginning on the sectors in which companies operate rather than on the location of their headquarters.

Information on sectors is given in the **FTSE Actuaries Share Indices** table (below the commentary), which shows the performance of the regional and sectoral indices in euro terms. Investors can also see indices that exclude those countries, such as the UK, that do not plan to join the single currency in the first wave.

A full breakdown of the stocks in the **FTSE Eurotop 300** index is given in the table that makes up the bottom left-hand quarter of the euro prices page. Prices and market capitalization are shown in euros.

The other leading indices that focus on continental Europe – the **Dow Jones Stoxx 50** and the **MSCI Europe** – are also published on the euro prices page.

But the single currency process has not just affected the equity markets. The page also shows the exchange rates of the euro against major world currencies, both on a spot (immediate delivery) basis and forward (delivery at some point in the future) basis.

As for the fixed income market, the creation of the euro has led to a single eurozone bond market, where investors focus less on the issuer's country of origin and more on its sector (e.g. whether it is a utility, or a sovereign borrower) and its rating by credit agencies. The table headed eurozone bonds focuses on representative bonds in each market category, and gives their latest price and yield, as well as the interest rate differential between them and benchmarket government bonds.

Dealing costs

There seems to be little way to avoid paying a higher charge for dealing in international stocks for the good reason that it costs more for the broker to buy them.

Killik charges 2.5 per cent on the first £10,000 of the deal (as opposed to 1.65 per cent for UK stocks), 1 per cent on the following £10,000 and 0.5 per cent after that.

The minimum charge is £75 (£40 for UK shares). There is also a £2.50 charge for dividend collection, against £1.50 in the UK.

Charles Schwab offers a dealing service for US stocks only. The minimum commission, which involves trading through its internet web site, comes out at £29.95, compared with the UK minimum on the same service of £15.

In current market circumstances, an overseas investment trust might be a much cheaper way of getting exposure to international companies. Of course, you have to pay an annual management fee and there is a bid-offer spread and commission costs.

But the key advantage is that you can buy many trusts at a steep discount to net asset values.

European trusts were trading in mid October 1998 at an average discount of 17.4 per cent; Japanese trusts at 23.9 per cent; and US trusts at 13.3 per cent.

For those who are bold enough to venture into emerging markets, the discount was a whopping 27.6 per cent.

There is nothing to say that these discounts cannot widen in the short term but the most likely reason for a widening would be a prolonged bear market – something that would be bad for investors whatever route they had chosen for investing internationally.

Furthermore, many specialist trusts have wind-up dates at which it is incumbent for fund managers to offer an exit route close to asset value.

For the long-term investor, therefore, a trust offers about the cheapest way to get international exposure, even if it does not provide the extra buzz available from directly owning shares in a company like IBM or Microsoft.

Now back in favour

Bonds used to form the bulk of a private investor's portfolio, but inflation saw them supplanted by equities. Now, after thirty years out of favour, they are suddenly a hot asset category. The assertion that the 1990s would be the decade of the bond has not been proved far wrong

Bonds have come back into fashion, After thirty years or more in which they were considered an investment category best left to the boring or the gullible, they are suddenly the hot asset category of the moment.

Their time has been coming for a while. The tide turned in favour of bonds in 1982 when Paul Volcker, then the chairman of the US Federal Reserve, started to cut interest rates, having decided he had won at least a temporary victory in the war against inflation. Then, after a further inflationary blip, in the late 1980s Norwich Union decreed that the 1990s would be the decade of the bond.

It was not far wrong. After the collapse in equity prices and surge in bonds that occurred in late summer 1998, the two asset categories had produced almost exactly equivalent returns over the course of the 1990s.

Once upon a time, bonds – instruments that offer to pay a (normally fixed) rate of interest for a fixed period – formed the bulk of a private investor's portfolio. Equities were regarded as a rather risky asset, not suitable for widows or orphans.

All that changed with the advent of the high inflation era of the 1960s and 1970s. Because the interest and repayment value of bonds is fixed in nominal terms, investors who held bonds saw the real value of their money fade away. With inflation at 5 per cent a year, the real value of money halves in fifteen years.

The key relationship in the bond market is between the interest rate paid on the bond and the bond's price; the former divided by the latter is the yield. As bond prices rise, yields fall and vice versa.

When inflation started to soar, investors pulled out of bonds in alarm and prices fell.

Or, looked at another way, they demanded a higher yield on their bonds as compensation for the effect of inflation. Either way, losses were substantial.

An investment of £1,000 in gilts (UK government bonds) in 1970, even with all the income reinvested free of tax, was worth just £682 in real terms by the end of the decade.

So rule number one of investing in the bond market is to watch out for inflation. If the market fears that inflation is reviving bond prices will quickly fall.

In the 1990s, it has been the apparent defeat of inflation that has allowed bonds to perform so well and yields to fall to their lowest level since the 1950s.

Deflation – that is, falling prices – should in most circumstances be good news for bonds. It means the real value of a fixed instrument such as a bond is constantly increasing. Yields can fall very low in nominal terms in such circumstances – in Japan, for example, they have dropped below 1 per cent. And 2 per cent bond yields were quite common in the century, when the price level over long periods was stable.

As a result of their obsession with inflation, bond investors are among the most misanthropic members of the financial community. They rejoice at news that shows the economy is slowing – falls in industrial production, increases in unemployment – which is unabashedly bad news for most members of the population.

But inflation is not the only factor affecting bonds. As with any other commodity, one has to pay attention to the balance of supply and demand.

In the bond market, one key component of supply is the amount of debt issued by governments, which in turn depends on the level of public spending deficits.

Until the advent of Keynesian economics, it was generally considered bad policy, except during wartime, for governments to run a deficit. As a result, government debt levels were quite a low proportion of gross domestic product.

After the Second World War, however, the adoption of demand-management techniques (boosting public spending to lift the economy out of recession) and the introduction of the welfare state led to substantial increases in government debt levels throughout the western world.

Even though governments in Europe and the US have taken action to cut their annual deficits in the 1990s, debt levels as a proportion of GDP remain high by historical standards. It is hard to see governments ever running big, or sustained, surpluses, to cut those ratios very far.

Fortunately for governments, the growth of life assurance and pension funds has provided a steady source of demand to soak up this supply. Bonds are a long-term asset with a dependable return (in nominal terms, at least) and provide a high level of income that can be useful for meeting the demands of pensioners.

And in the UK recent changes in pension legislation, designed to ensure funds have adequate resources to meet their run, should lead to increased holdings of gilts.

For private investors, the attractions of gilts are security (if the UK government cannot pay its debts, the country really is in a mess), a high income (or at least a higher income than on equities) and tax-free capital gains.

But there are drawbacks, quite apart from the danger that inflation might return. The first is that, at current market levels, the yield on gilts is below that prevailing on cash (and available from, say, a money-market unit trust). Thus investors are having to give up current income to buy gilts.

The second is that the vast majority of gilt issues trade above their issue prices. That means an investor who buys a gilt and holds it until the repayment date is locking in a capital loss, and a loss, furthermore, that is not offsettable for tax purposes against gains elsewhere. One answer is to buy undated gilts such as Consols or War Loans, that trade well below their par value (for the good reason that they will never be repaid).

But these issues have had a very good run, and the easy money may have been made already.

SHOULD I INVEST IN BONDS?

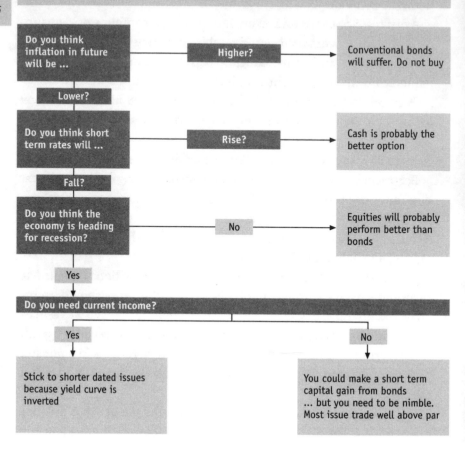

Could gilt yields fall, and prices rise, further? They could, without postulating the Japanese deflationary example. With ten-year gilts yielding around 5 per cent and inflation around 2.5 per cent, the real yield on bonds is 2.5 per cent. That is around the average level for real yields from the 1930s to the 1960s. So a fall in inflation to, say, 2 per cent leaves some scope for nominal yields to drop to 4.5 per cent.

Furthermore, the UK government has to pay a higher yield on its bonds than the German administration because of the risk that sterling will depreciate over the longer term (which it has, all too often, in the past). Should the UK join up for the European single currency, however, that foreign exchange risk would disappear and gilt yields could drop to German levels, as they have in other devaluation-prone countries such as Italy and Spain.

But gilts are not the only bond market choice for the private investor. Many other entities, such as blue-chip companies or supranational organizations such as the World Bank, issue bonds.

The risk-reward principle of finance holds here. The less credit-worthy the organization, the higher the yield investors will demand. People who are searching for a better income than gilts can provide have to choose how much risk they are willing to accept.

The very riskiest credits tend to be known as 'junk bonds', a market that flourished in the 1980s as investors became persuaded that, provided one held a diversified portfolio of such assets, the higher yield would more than compensate for the risk involved.

During bull markets, as investors become more confident about accepting risk, the spread (in terms of higher yield) that poor credit risks have to pay over government bonds steadily reduces. Then, the market is jolted by some bad news that widens the spread all over again (and causes the prices of bonds with poor credit risks to fall).

One such jolt came in December 1994 when Mexico, having assured investors it would do no such thing, devalued the peso. Another came in August 1998, when Russia effectively defaulted on its debt. It was this latter event, which caused spreads to widen very sharply, that caused so much pain to the US hedge fund, Long-Term Capital Management.

For the private investor buying individual bonds, avoiding risk would seem to be the highest priority, especially in current economic circumstances. So, despite the higher yields on offer, it would seem sensible to concentrate on the blue-chip end of the corporate market.

Another option is to go overseas and buy other countries' government bonds. But this is not an easy answer – it involves currency risk and in most cases pays a lower yield than is available in the UK. And there is no relief from capital gains tax on overseas government bond holdings, either.

Furthermore, the recent effective default by Russia illustrates that overseas government bonds do not offer that much security. While one might reasonably rely on the UK government to repay its internal debt, other governments have frequently defaulted or suspended payments – several times in Latin America, and once before in Russia, when the Communists refused to honour Tsarist debt.

And there is not much that outside investors can do if a government refuses to honour its debt. Legal action will presumably fail in the country itself and courts outside that country will have no power to enforce their decisions.

If individuals fail to keep up their mortgage payments, their houses can be repossessed by the building society, but one can hardly repossess Russia.

That said, there are many governments where default is pretty unthinkable. The US Treasury bond market is the most liquid in the world and is often used as a safe haven by international investors.

Most European governments can also be seen as reliable payers but their bonds could fall into a Catch 22 category. If the UK does not sign up for the euro, sterling investors will face a currency risk; but if the UK does sign up, yields and prices of gilts and European bonds will move in line so there may not be much point.

VIEWPOINT

Further to go

One of the most bullish supporters of the bond market recently has been, appropriately enough, Tim Bond, director of rate strategy at Barclays Capital. He believes the US thirty-year Treasury bond could fall to 3.5 per cent and that UK gilt yields could drop below 4 per cent.

Bond believes that the world has gone through a phase of excessive investment that has produced a lot of spare capacity. That pushes down output prices of goods and services and will reduce inflation. The result will be that companies will not borrow for investment and the supply of new bonds will fall.

Although governments may increase their spending in response to recessionary forces, that will take some time to feed through to the markets. The effect of debt redemption and high coupon payments should mean that investors have enough cashflow to absorb new supply.

At the same time as the supply of bonds is shrinking, demand will be increasing, says Bond. The primary factor is demographic – the ratio of workers and savers, relative to the very young and very old, is very high. The result is a surplus of labour, putting downward pressure on wages, and an abundance of savers.

In the US, the savings ratio has been low. In recent years investors have felt that the market was saving for them. Now that the stock market appears to have turned, US investors will be forced to save more, depressing consumption and adding a disinflationary pressure on the economy.

All this favours bonds, says Bond, who is not abashed by the mid-October 1998 setback in the bond markets, which he sees as an overdue technical correction, partly prompted by enforced hedge fund selling.

HOW THE FT CAN HELP

Gilts prices

Understanding gilts can be difficult but the *FT*'s **gilts table** on the international capital markets page is a useful guide.

The first thing to understand is that gilt yields and prices have an inverse relationship (see above) and so a fall in prices will mean a rise in yields on the day.

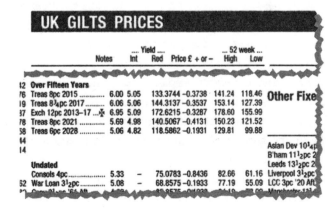

		Yield			52 week	
	Notes	Int	Red	Price £ + or –	High	Low
12	**Over Fifteen Years**					
76	Treas 8pc 2015	6.00	5.05	133.3744 –0.3738	141.24	118.46
19	Treas 8¼pc 2017	6.06	5.06	144.3137 –0.3537	153.14	127.39
37	Exch 12pc 2013–17 ...✗	6.95	5.09	172.6215 –0.3287	178.60	155.99
78	Treas 8pc 2021	5.69	4.98	140.5067 –0.4131	150.23	121.52
58	Treas 6pc 2028	5.06	4.82	118.5862 –0.1931	129.81	99.88
44						
14						
	Undated					
	Consols 4pc	5.33	–	75.0783 –0.8436	82.66	61.16
52	War Loan 3½pc	5.08	–	68.8575 –0.1933	77.19	55.09

UK GILTS PRICES

Other Fixe

Asian Dev 10¼p
B'ham 11½pc 2
Leeds 13½pc 2
Liverpool 3½pc
LCC 3pc '20 Aft

The second thing to realize is that there are two types of gilt yields (both of which are given in the table) – interest (or running) and gross redemption, which appear as 'Int' and 'Red' to save space.

The interest yield calculates the interest on the bond as a percentage of the market price and thus represents the current income available to the investor.

The gross redemption yield introduces a second factor into the equation – the capital gain or loss if the bond is held until maturity.

In most cases at the moment gilts trade at a price greater than their repayment value (generally £100) and thus a new investor is locking in a capital loss if he hangs on to the bond.

As a consequence, gross redemption yields are lower than running yields. On 30 October 1998, for example, the 9 per cent Treasury 2008 traded at £130.495 −0.2897. Its running yield was a healthy 6.9 per cent. But a new investor would be locking in a capital loss of £30 for gross yield of only 5 per cent.

The table lists the gilt issues, grouped by maturity date, with the shortest-lived issues (under five years) appearing first. The repayment date of each issue is given, together with the original interest rate.

Very short issues are in effect money market instruments and thus have a yield close to the prevailing base, or repo rate. Short dated issues also trade close to their repayment price; who would want to pay £110 for a bond for which they will receive just £100 in six months?

Yields on longer-dated issues will depend, among other things, on expectations on inflation and short-term interest rates.

Normally long-dated gilts will have a higher yield than short-dated issues because investors expect a reward in return for tying up their money for a long period (just as you get money in a sixty- or ninety-day notice account). This is known as a positive-sloping yield curve.

But, in current market circumstances, long-dated yields are well below short rates – an inverted yield curve. This is because the Bank of England has raised short rates substantially to counter an inflationary threat; the market evidently expects the Bank to succeed in fighting inflation and for rates to eventually be brought down again.

One section of the market, undated gilts, will never be repaid (in spite of government promises on War Loans). Since they will never be repaid, they do not have a redemption yield; all were issued at rates well below current market levels and continue to trade well below their face value.

Index-linked gilt prices are also listed with other sterling bonds, many of which were issued by local authorities such as Birmingham and Leeds. On the same page, investors can find the prices and yields of bonds issued by **other governments**.

TOP TIP

Gilt strips

Gilt strips offer a new investment opportunity for the UK private investor, although one that will have to be treated carefully.

The strips market was only introduced in December 1997, although it has long been a feature of the US bond industry. A strip separates a bond into its component parts – one for each interest payment (known as a coupon strip) and one that receives the repayment value (a principal strip).

The attraction of any strip is that it delivers a good deal of certainty. The repayment level is known in advance, just like a zero coupon bond; the investor buys the strip at a discount to the face value. In effect, all the return is received right at the end.

This has an obvious appeal for those investing for a specific long-term purpose – for example, to pay for school or college fees. The problem is that, until now, the tax treatment has been unappealing; the Inland Revenue has taxed the annual notional gains on strips even though the investor has not received an income.

This has changed with the introduction of Individual Savings Accounts (ISAs) in April 1999. Most gilts can be held directly in an ISA, provided that the issues have at least five years to go until maturity when bought. As yet the government says strips can only be held via a collective investment scheme, but it is considering pleas for strips to be eligible to be held directly. Holding via an ISA means the strips can grow tax free; holding directly would eliminate unnecessary management costs.

Strips are available that mature on 7 June or 7 December every year between now and December 2028.

The further the repayment date, the lower the current price per £100 nominal. In late October 1998, the principal strip due to be redeemed on 7 December 2000 was trading at just under £90 per £100; the one due to be redeemed on 7 December 2028 at £25 per £100.

Investors also need to be aware that strips can fluctuate quite sharply in price as they are very sensitive to changes in interest rate expectations.

Guarding against inflation

For the risk-averse, index-linked gilts are often a sound investment choice. But current economic conditions are not ideal and 'linkers' look rather expensive. You may find that the cost of extra security outweighs the 'comfort factor' these investments can offer

They seemed a good idea when launched in 1981 amid the inflationary ruins of the 1970s. But do index-linked gilts make any sense for the private investor today? After all, today's talk is of disinflation (slowing inflation) or even outright deflation (price falls).

Certainly the Bank of England is pursuing the development of the inflation-proofed government bond sector with some gusto. It is worth some £60bn, about a quarter the size of the conventional (or fixed-interest) gilt market. There is now a full range of maturity dates – a dozen issues have terms to redemption of anywhere between one and thirty-two years – and there has been a substantial demand recently, mainly from pension funds keen to match their liabilities to pay pensions that are partly or fully indexed to future inflation. Life assurance companies also buy 'linkers' in order to repackage them as index-linked annuities.

Curiously, as global inflation has declined, the concept of inflation-proofing has become more popular around the world. The US Treasury introduced Treasury Inflation Protected Securities (TIPS) and the French Treasury followed with the launch of a ten-year indexed Obligation Assimilable du Trésor (the 'OATi' for short) as a benchmark for this class of investment within the eurozone.

Investors need to be careful, because these governments are not issuing indexed bonds out of the goodness of their hearts but because they think they will reduce their cost of borrowing.

When Nigel Lawson issued the first index-linked gilts in 1981 he did so in the face of stiff resistance from the Bank of England. But he much later explained his reasons: that linkers would be saleable when conventional fixed-interest gilts were not, and also that future inflation would be lower than investors expected, so the linkers would prove to be a cheap way of funding the government's debts.

He proved to be right on both counts. Eager investors bought the first issue on a real yield of 2 per cent, and they lost money as the yield drifted up (and thus the indexed gilt prices fell) through the 1980s. Experience has shown that a 'normal' real yield can be regarded as between perhaps 3 and 4 per cent. The highest ever was nearly 5 per cent in the dark days just before the UK left the European exchange rate mechanism in 1992. Recently the real yield has been about 3 per cent, which is on the low side.

Index-linked government bonds are about the safest long-term investments you can buy. The credit risk is minimal, for countries such as the UK, the US and France, anyway. The inflation risk is taken away, too. In exchange for being insured against this inflation risk investors will accept a lower real yield, which is why governments find this kind of bond is particularly cheap to issue in normal circumstances. Like other gilts, linkers can be bought and sold through the Post Office, or through brokers.

Over the 10 years ended 1997 the annualized gross total return on index-linked gilts was 9.7 per cent; on conventional gilts it was 12.0 per cent; and on UK equities it was 15.7 per cent. Theory suggests, however, that the differentials will normally be smaller than in that particular period.

Linkers do bear an interest rate risk, however, which can be quite substantial for the longer-dated issues. A fall in real yields from, say, 3½ to 2½ per cent will generate a very substantial price change. This is almost exactly what happened between mid-1997 and mid-1998, after which period some longs were showing year-on-year capital gains of 30 per cent. If yields were to move the other way there would be similar capital losses. These fluctuations are much smaller on shorter-dated issues, however.

Index-linked gilts have a useful role in long-term personal portfolios as safe, core holdings. A real return of 3 per cent may not sound very much, but it will compound to a doubled real value over twenty-five years (assuming that income is reinvested). Higher-rate taxpayers have found index-linked gilts attractive in the past, because most of the nominal total return is tax-free. As both inflation and nominal interest rates fall, however, this advantage becomes less significant.

Compared with conventional gilts, linkers offer the assurance that their real value will not be wiped out by inflation, a fate substantially suffered by fixed-interest bonds after the Second World War. Also, compared with equities, they offer protection against the risk of an economic slump. However, equities can normally be expected to give a significantly higher return.

Linkers will do well when there is an unexpected burst of high inflation. Ironically, they may also perform quite strongly in depression-type conditions when real interest rates are falling (though ordinary gilts may do even better in these circumstances). Index-linked gilts will be less satisfactory investments, however, in benign conditions of moderate economic growth and steady inflation. In these circumstances investors will not be able to make much of a claim against the inflation insurance premium they are effectively paying and will miss out on the benefits of economic growth for equities.

Index-linked National Savings Certificates provide an alternative to index-linked gilts. The latest issue offers 2 per cent real income, but only if held for the bonus after five years. Allowing for standard rate tax on the coupon, the real return on index-linked gilts is about the same. The gilts offer greater liquidity, in that they can be sold at any time, without an automatic penalty, but there is a risk of capital loss. Smaller savers will probably find the certificates more convenient. On page 139, we explain how to choose between the two.

How do index-linked gilts work? Both the coupon (the interest income, paid half-yearly) and the principal are indexed to the Retail Price Index. However, for technical reasons related to the gilt market's need to know the next half-yearly interest payment precisely, and delays in the availability of each month's RPI, there is an eight-month lag in indexation. (See chart for the sums.) In effect, inflation protection ceases at eight months from maturity.

HOW TO DO INDEX-LINKED SUMS

Information needed

- Name of stock 4 $^1/_8$ per cent Index-Linked **Treasury Stock 2030**
- When first issued **12 June 1992**
- Interest payment dates **22 January and 22 July**
- Redemption date **22 July 2030**
- Eight months before stock first issued (base month for calculations) **October 1991**
- Next interest payment **January 1999**
- Eight months before date of interest payment **May 1998**
- Eight months before redemption date **November 2029**
- Half-yearly interest payment per £100 (half annual coupon) **£4.125 ÷ 2 = £2.0625**
- Retail Price Index (RPI) for October 1991 **135.1**
- RPI for May 1998 **163.5**
- Estimated RPI for November 2029 **342.9** (assumes inflation of 2.5 per cent per year)

Calculating interest payments and estimating principal repayments

Actual interest payment on 22 January 1999

Half-yearly interest payment x (RPI eight months before payment ÷ RPI in base month) **£2.0625 x (163.5 ÷ 135.1) = £2.496 per £100 nominal of stock**

Estimated principal repayment in July 2030

Nominal capital x (estimated RPI eight months before redemption ÷ RPI in base month) **£100 x (342.9 ÷ 135.1) = £253.8119**

Investors and the economic cycle

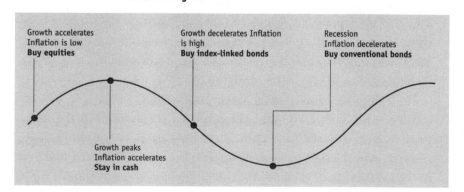

Growth accelerates
Inflation is low
Buy equities

Growth decelerates Inflation is high
Buy index-linked bonds

Recession
Inflation decelerates
Buy conventional bonds

Growth peaks
Inflation accelerates
Stay in cash

Idealized cycle: in practice, distortion may occur and time lags will vary

What about the possibility of deflation? Holders of index-linked gilts would not be any worse off in real terms, but their income and capital would be falling in nominal terms. They would be much better off in fixed-interest gilts in those circumstances. But we have not had a year of falling prices in the UK since the Second World War.

The fundamental value of index-linked gilts from time to time can be assessed relative to conventional gilts. At present the conventional yield is about 5 per cent, some 2.5 per cent more than for linkers. The gap represents the break-even inflation rate that would equalize the returns from the two varieties of gilts. But it includes the inflation risk premium which cannot be independently determined but is often assumed to be about 0.5 per cent.

This leaves perhaps 2 per cent as the implied market expectation of long-run inflation. Is this realistic? After all, the Bank of England's central target rate is 2.5 per cent. It does rather look as though the real yield on linkers is somewhat low at present, perhaps because of heavy buying by pension funds for technical reasons connected with the minimum funding requirement imposed by the Pensions Act 1995. Also, the supply from the government is subdued at present, but will expand if there is a recession. Long-term investors might do well to wait for a better buying opportunity.

There is some confirmation from overseas markets. The real yield on TIPS is about 3.8 per cent and on the OATi 3.1 per cent. There are problems in making exact comparisons with UK yields because of slight differences in the design of the bonds. Also, these foreign linker markets are newer and may be less liquid. All the same, several UK institutions have recently been buying TIPS rather than UK linkers. This introduces a short-term currency risk, however: in the very long term, national inflation differentials will offset exchange rate changes, but this certainly cannot be relied on over periods of a few years.

Linkers are of value to risk-averse investors. Personal investors have other ways of protecting themselves against inflation, however – through property and equities, for instance.

Historically, investors in index-linked government bonds have paid a high opportunity cost to avoid the inflation risk (though they have done very well in the past six years).

In some respects, index-linked government bonds today fulfil the role of gold in a nineteenth-century investment portfolio.

In normal circumstances, linkers will lag behind other, more exciting, investments. Just occasionally, however, perhaps only once in a generation, you will be very glad indeed that they are there.

INDEXED PENSIONS

Expensive choice

Many people want to protect their pensions against inflation. Civil service pensions are inflation-proofed, and some members of company pension schemes also have some degree of inflation-proofing to their pensions. A good scheme might offer annual increases at the rate of 5 per cent a year or the RPI, whichever was the lower.

But people with money purchase company schemes or personal pensions have to buy their own inflation-proofing, and it does not come cheap. In both cases the pensioner has not built up an entitlement to a specific pension during his working life; he has built up ownership of an investment fund which he uses to buy an annuity – an income for life – when he retires.

The income he can expect will depend partly on his age (the younger you are, the lower it will normally be) and partly on any other conditions. If, for example, a pensioner wants his wife to continue to get a pension when he dies, his pension will be less than if it died with him.

Similarly, if he wants to inflation-proof his retirement income, his initial income is lower than it would be if he opted for a 'level annuity', which would pay the same amount year after year. Indeed, it is a lot lower. A sixty-year-old man retiring today would get around 40 per cent less if he chose either an annuity with annual increases of 5 per cent or one linked to the RPI. For a 65-year-old the reduction in immediate income would be 35 per cent. That is a hefty cut particularly since basic annuity rates have been declining recently.

● A handful of companies and building societies have issued RPI-linked loans. But they have ceased to be attractive to most private investors since the last government made the whole of the return taxable.

Gilt issues table

The obvious alternative to index-linked gilts is index-linked National Savings certificates. Both are issued by the UK government; both protect the holder against inflation. And most advisers recommend holding both. But what are the comparative attractions?

■ Gilt issues – best value v tax status

Your capital gain on a gilt – a UK government bond – is tax free. However, you pay tax on the interest. Therefore, gilts which deliver a higher proportion of their total return as capital gains

40% TAXPAYERS		Stock	Price	Yield %	Volatility %
				2.21§§	
CONVENTIONAL	<5yr	Treasury 6.00%, 1999	99 28/32	3.71	0.77%
	5-10yr	Treasury 6.75%, 2004	108 29/32	2.46	5.34%
	10-15yr	Treasury 5.75%, 2009	105 28/32	2.83	9.18%
	>15yr	Treasury 6.00%, 2028	116 16/32	2.79	19.04%
INDEX-LINKED		Index-Lnkd 2.5%, 2001	203 26/32	5.13♣	2.78%
				1.92§§	
		Index-Lnkd 2%, 2006	222 12/32	5.00♣	7.20%
				1.80§§	

Yield is redemption yield and takes account of any change in the capital value over period to maturity. Volatility is a measure of the sensitivity of the stock price to changes in yield. ♣Money yield (current inflation assumed). §§Real yield (adjusted for inflation).   Source: Barclays Capital

Three tables in Weekend Money on Saturdays help you do some rough sums. They are **gilt issues – best value vs tax status; best deposit rates**; and the **Moneywatch table**, which includes the Retail Price Index.

● **Basic characteristics.** The gilts offer a greater range of investment periods if you want to lock your money away; the certificates are a fixed five-year term.

Gilts can be sold whenever you choose, but if you sell before they mature you are exposed to the risk of adverse stock market price movements, particularly if inflation falls. The certificates cannot decrease in value and involve no market risk, though there will be reductions in the normal returns if you want your money back early.

The gilts pay interest twice a year; the whole of the return on the certificates comes at the end.

There are commission charges on gilts but not on National Savings.

● **Taxation.** Both index-linked savings certificates and index-linked gilts tend to appeal most to high taxpayers. The certificates are tax-free and produce the same returns to all investors, regardless of their tax status.

For the high taxpayer these returns are often attractive compared with what he can get on conventional investments. But non-taxpayers or those who pay basic rate tax can often find better value in conventional investments.

The same reasoning applies to a lesser extent with index-linked gilts. Income is taxable, but the exemption from capital gains tax on these stocks includes official increases in repayment values to compensate for inflation. Thus a smaller proportion of the total return on an index-linked stock is taxable compared with returns on conventional stocks.

● **A quick and dirty way** to compare probable returns.

(We used the 24 October 1998 *FT*.) Take the real return offered by the certificates – 2 per cent – and add the inflation rate – 3.2 per cent. (The first figure is in the **best deposit rates** table; the RPI is in the **Moneywatch table**.) The total – 5.2 per cent – is the nominal tax-free return you would get on the certificates if inflation stayed at the same level for five years.

Now you need the comparable figure for a five-year index-linked gilt for someone in your tax bracket. Weekend Money's weekly **gilts table** gives it. Say your marginal tax rate is 40 per cent. We quote a couple of linkers with different redemption dates: index-linked 2.5 per cent 2001, which had a nominal net redemption yield of 5.1 per cent assuming current inflation, or index-linked 2 per cent 2006, with a comparable yield of 5 per cent. The certificates look marginally more attractive than the gilts, but there was not much to choose between them. For non-taxpayers or basic rate taxpayers, the linkers won.

It is worth doing the comparison afresh whenever you are considering buying. The relationship between the two returns is not constant.

Buying gilts

There are three ways of buying gilts:

- direct from the Debt Management Office when a new stock is issued
- from the market
- from the Bank of England brokerage service.

The first way is cheapest but of limited application; the second is fastest; the third is usually cheaper but slower than the second.

THERE ARE THREE ACCEPTED WAYS OF BUYING GILTS. 'FROM A BLOKE YOU MET IN THE PUB' IS NOT ONE OF THEM

ROGER BEALE

When the Bank is issuing a new stock, or a large slug of an existing stock, it usually does so by auction, with the details announced in advance. You can go on to a mailing list for new issues by calling the Registrar's department (01452–398080). No commission is payable, but you may well find that only a minority of the offers are of interest. Professional investors enter competitive bids for the stock, and private investors can do so too. But most will probably prefer to make non-competitive bids – in which case they pay whatever the average price paid by competitive bidders is.

You can buy or sell existing gilts through a stockbroker, just like shares. This will normally mean that you can deal straight away knowing the price you will get. Alternatively some brokers will allow you to set a price limit – which means they will only deal if the price gets to this pre-agreed level. Charges vary, though they are normally lower than on shares. Some brokers have a fixed price; others operate a sliding scale, which might start at, say, 1.25 per cent on the first £15,000 for deals above their minimum.

The Bank of England's dealing service used to be known as the National Savings Stock Register. The service is usually a cheaper route for investing in gilts, though one reader wrote in to say that on a deal worth £100,000 his broker was actually cheaper than the Bank. But purchases and sales must be made by post. Forms are available from the post office, by telephone (0800–818614) or through the internet (http://www.BANKOFENGLAND.CO.UK). The Bank does not undertake to buy at a particular price on a particular day, so there is some risk in volatile market conditions.

Managed funds vs going it alone

Buying gilts directly is better than using gilt funds. But, when it comes to corporate bonds, managed funds have some merits

Bond funds are a large and stable part of the US mutual fund market, representing around a quarter of investors' assets. But, in the UK, the sector has never achieved anything like that kind of popularity in spite of growth in recent years.

The problem with bond funds in the UK has been twofold. First, bonds themselves were not a very attractive investment in the 1970s and much of the 1980s, thanks to the severe effects of inflation. And even in the bond-friendly 1990s, investors who wanted a fixed-income product have had alternatives in the form of permanent income-bearing shares from building societies, fixed-rate ISAs or National Savings bonds.

Second, bond fund managers attach charges to their funds that reduce their attractions. Annual fees vary from 0.5 per cent to 1.6 per cent and initial charges from nil to 5.75 per cent. These can make quite a dent in the investor's income at any time, but the effect is even more marked in low-yield times when gilts are yielding just 5 per cent or so.

When it comes to owning gilts, it is a particular struggle for investors to justify paying such fees. Gilt prices and yields are easy to find; the credit rating of the UK government is scarcely a matter for debate; and there is a simple and cheap way of buying gilts via a form available at the Post Office. Furthermore, gilts held for your own account are free of capital gains tax, but any profits made from a bond fund are taxable.

Nor can fund managers claim any particular expertise in outperforming the market. The average UK gilt fund rose 39.6 per cent

BONDS vs EQUITIES – O'HIGGINS METHOD

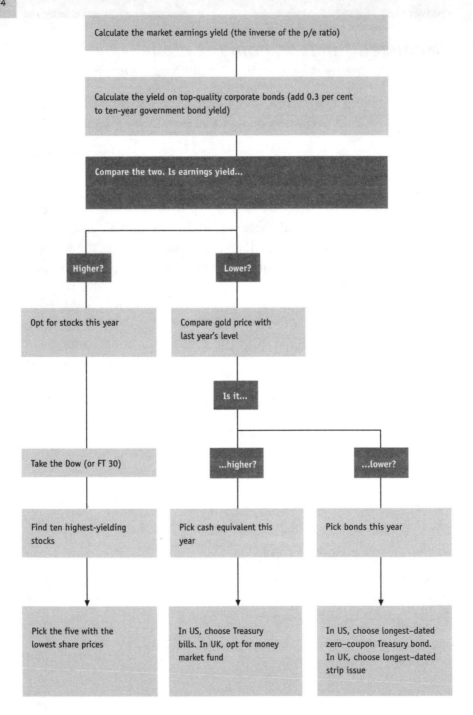

Calculate the market earnings yield (the inverse of the p/e ratio)

Calculate the yield on top-quality corporate bonds (add 0.3 per cent to ten-year government bond yield)

Compare the two. Is earnings yield...

Higher?

Lower?

Opt for stocks this year

Compare gold price with last year's level

Is it...

Take the Dow (or FT 30)

...higher?

...lower?

Find ten highest-yielding stocks

Pick cash equivalent this year

Pick bonds this year

Pick the five with the lowest share prices

In US, choose Treasury bills. In UK, opt for money market fund

In US, choose longest–dated zero–coupon Treasury bond. In UK, choose longest–dated strip issue

Earnings yield on FTSE All–Share index
per cent

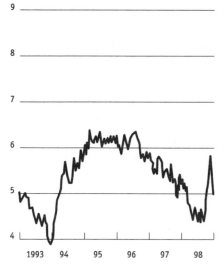

UK ten–year benchmark bond yield
per cent

Gold bullion
$ per troy ounce

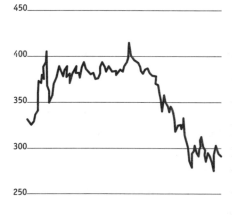

FT–30 highest–yielding shares

Name	Dividend yield, per cent	Price (pence)
BTR	**10.00**	**109**
P&O Dfd	6.15	620
ICI	5.34	599
British Airways	**5.25**	**405**
Allied Domecq	4.91	516
Royal and Sun Alliance	4.79	493
Tate and Lyle	**4.72**	**360**
EMI	**4.48**	**357**
NatWest	4.35	960
Scottish Power	4.32	610
Blue Circle	**4.32**	**340**

Source: Datastream/ICV

Share price and dividend yields at 10 November 1998

(excluding the initial charge) over the five years to 1 October 1998; that compares with a total return from the J.P. Morgan UK government bond index of 62.7 per cent. This is not quite such a bad performance as it might seem – the index does not take account of tax – but, even allowing for that factor, funds are well behind.

International bond funds offer diversification away from the UK, but have no tax advantages, present a currency risk, and, at the moment, offer a lower yield than is available on gilts. The near-default in Russia and the financial crisis in many emerging markets in 1998 are also reminders that there is a substantial credit risk involved in owning overseas bonds.

Owning corporate bond funds, however, seems to make more sense for the private investor. This is an area where expertise is much more useful, in terms of assessing credit risk and the technicalities of different issues; and prices are not so accessible as they are for gilts.

Corporate bond funds offered ISA investors an attractive tax-free income, especially as the government is gradually whittling away the tax privileges of equities. From April 1999, and the introduction of ISAs, the tax credit attached to equities fell to 10 per cent, and it will go altogether in 2004.

Even after the recent fall in equity prices, shares still yield only about 2.5 per cent gross: not much of an income return for investors. And, while some equity fund managers still manage to offer a higher yield, the performance of the high-yield sector of the stock market has not been encouraging in recent years. So those who use PEPs for income may want a sizeable bond fund element.

Bond funds also provide a bolt-hole for investors when they feel world equity markets are overvalued. Cash can only be held in a PEP for a short time without attracting the wrath of the Inland Revenue; selling out of the PEP will mean the allowance for that year is lost for ever. A switch out of equities into bonds in June 1998, for example, would have more than justified any charges incurred.

The diversification argument for owning bonds has taken rather a battering in recent years. Analysts have pointed out that equities and bonds have tended to move together, but with equities outperforming: the optimal level of bonds within a portfolio is thus zero. And the mar-

gin by which shares have beaten bonds over the long run is phenomenal; £1,000 invested in 1945 would by the end of 1997 have grown, with
gross income reinvested, to £737,000 in the former and £25,000 in
the latter.

But the recent downturn in world stock markets, which was accompanied by a surge in bond prices, indicates that there are times in the
economic cycle when bonds can outperform markedly.

A low-inflation, low-growth world may be one in which the difference in performance between equities and bonds may be much less
marked than it was. So far in the 1990s, the performance of the two UK
categories has been virtually neck and neck.

There has been some sign in recent months that bonds are being re-
rated relative to equities, and this may be a long-term shift. A bond
yield/equity yield ratio of 2 may have been appropriate in a high-
inflation era, but back before 1959 equities actually yielded more than
bonds because of their perceived higher risk.

While few believe that the latter situation will recur, it may be that
bonds will be a better diversification than they have been in the past.

In the US, one traditional rule of thumb is that bonds should make
up a proportion of your portfolio that is equivalent to your age. So a
thirty-year-old should have only 30 per cent on bonds and a seventy-
year-old, with a greater need for income, 70 per cent in bonds and so on.

The above is a rather conservative approach (and it is probably inap-
propriate, for tax reasons, for a thirty-year-old UK citizen to have such
a high proportion in fixed income) but the general principle that
the older the investor, the larger the bond element of the portfolio, is
worth noting.

It is also worth noting that gilt and corporate bond funds do not
always move in line. The recent turmoil in financial markets has caused
investors to flee all kinds of risks and to prefer high-quality government
bonds to corporate debt. Many corporate borrowers have seen yields
rise (and prices fall), in spite of the good climate for government bonds.

But even after you have decided to invest in a bond fund, picking a
fund is still a fairly complex matter.

The advertised yield can be an area of confusion. Some bonds trum-
pet the running (interest) yield – the immediate income available as a

proportion of the unit price. But this may be misleading. The underlying bonds within the portfolio may well have been bought well above their face value, and thus may have a much lower gross redemption, than running, yield. Eventually, the managers will face a capital loss on their portfolios, which means that, by paying out a high immediate running yield, they are in effect running down investors' capital.

The same caveat also applies to the annual charge. A fund that takes its annual charge out of capital will appear to have a higher yield than one that takes the charge out of income. But investors who opt for that higher yield are eating into their capital and therefore their future income-producing ability.

With more than two-thirds of corporate bond funds having a record of less than three years, charges are a pretty important method of distinguishing between trusts. Around seventeen have an annual charge of less than 1 per cent (Threadneedle charges just 0.5 per cent, with a 2 per cent initial fee); about ten funds, including M&G and Virgin, have no initial charge.

PROFILE

Corporate specialist

Paul Reed has been working in the bond markets for fifty years and has been managing the Aberdeen Prolific Fixed Interest Fund (under its various names) since 1991.

The recent turbulence in bond markets, which saw government bonds surge in price but debt issued by more risky corporates take a battering, was the most volatile market he has seen in a decade. 'Russia was the first domino and then we saw hedge funds, who thought they had seen a low-risk opportunity in corporate debt, pull out in the face of margin calls,' he says.

The fund switched from being a gilt and fixed-interest trust in the early 1990s and has since concentrated on corporate debt, particularly convertibles, where Reed says one can often get a higher yield than from gilts, plus a chance of some upside if the shares perform well.

The tactic has worked well, putting the fund first in its sector over both seven and ten years, but the market turned against him in the autumn, leaving the fund the worst performer of the sector in September.

However, investors, encouraged by the tax relief given to corporate bond funds under the personal equity plan rules, continued to pour money into the fund. That has allowed Reed to buy some debt at what he sees as tempting prices. The Individual Savings Account rules, which reduce the tax credit on equities but not on bonds, have continued to encourage private investors to back the sector.

HOW THE FT CAN HELP

Managed funds

Investors seeking a fund manager to look after their assets are not exactly short of choice. Six pages at the back of the second section of the *Financial Times* are filled with listings of **managed funds**.

The section is split roughly into three. The first deals with UK-based unit trusts and open-ended investment companies (OEICs). Funds are grouped by fund manager, with the address and phone number shown for each group.

The individual funds are then listed, with the initial, or front end, charge shown in percentage terms. Unit trusts then show the selling and

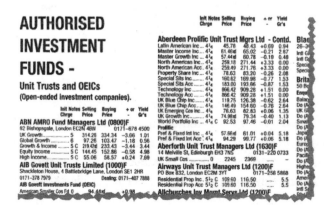

buying, or bid and offer, prices, whereas OEICs have just one price.

It is important to remember that this is not as great a distinction as it might seem. The difference between the bid and offer prices for a unit trust contains the initial charge, whereas, for an OEIC investor, the charge is added on separately.

So a unit trust might have a bid price of 99.75p and an offer price of 105p, with an initial charge of 5 per cent. If you bought at the offer price of 105p and immediately sold at the bid price of 99.75 per cent you would be 5 per cent worse off; with an OEIC you would buy and sell at the same price but would have to pay an initial charge.

The last two columns show the unit price change on the previous day and the gross income yield.

Details are also given of whether the manager deals at a historic or forward pricing (shown as H or F after the company name). If the former, the manager will deal at a declared price (which may be the one published in the paper); in the latter, investors are not given a definite price in advance.

The second section shows the various insurance funds available, which broadly split into two; life funds (such as unit-linked endowment policies) and personal pension funds. These are funds whose prices are useful for those trying to value their policies. Once again, there is normally a buying and selling price, with the spread between the two largely reflecting management charges.

Offshore funds have their own large section, with funds split both by domicile and by how they are regulated. Some funds are 'recognized' by the Financial Services Authority (FSA), which means they can be sold into the UK and, accordingly, must have investor protection and regulations that are equivalent.

The good news is that in Bermuda, Guernsey, the Isle of Man and Jersey, recognized funds qualify for investor compensation schemes; the bad news, for the adventurous, is that such funds are more restricted in where and how they can invest.

The world of offshore funds is rather more complicated than that onshore. Sometimes funds will have different classes of share; sometimes they will have umbrellas that make it easy to switch from one type of fund to another.

Charges, particularly annual or recurring fees, tend to be higher in the offshore market and, in some cases, regulation is not as severe. It also can be harder to get information; many offshore managers do not put their address or phone number in the *FT*. Remember also that the tax advantages of investing offshore are pretty limited these days.

Shares vs bonds

Finding a system for timing the market is one of the holy grails of investment. But the prize has been claimed by Michael O'Higgins, the US fund manager whose high-yield stockpicking system has been featured many times in the personal finance pages of the *FT*.

The system, which is outlined in a forthcoming book (*Beating the Dow with Bonds*, HarperBusiness), is designed for the US investor but could be adapted for the UK. The investor is faced at the start of the year with three choices: shares, Treasury bills or a long-dated Treasury bond.

To compare shares with the other two assets, first work out the earnings yield on the index (the inverse of the price/earnings ratio). So if the p/e on the market is 20, the earnings yield is 5 per cent.

Then compare that with the yield on top-rated corporate bonds (O'Higgins suggests taking the yield on the ten-year Treasury bond and adding 30 basis points, or 0.3 per cent. UK investors could substitute gilts for T-bond yields). If the earnings yield is higher than the bond yield, choose stocks.

Stocks are selected by their own system; of the ten highest-yielding stocks in the index, take the five with the lowest nominal price. O'Higgins uses the Dow, UK investors could use the FT-30.

If the earnings yield is below the bond yield, then investors still have to choose between bonds and Treasury bills. O'Higgins says the key element is the price of gold; if it is higher than its level a year before, choose the T-bill (UK investors could opt for a low-charging money-market fund); if it is lower, choose the bond.

But O'Higgins opts for the zero coupon Treasury bond, the most geared way of playing the bond market. For UK investors, the equivalent strategy would be to buy the longest-dated gilt strip available, which is currently 2028.

O'Higgins claims this strategy (which would only have picked stocks in seven years) would have earned 23.8 per cent a year since 1969, higher than the 11.7 per cent return on the Dow.

Choosing the vehicle that suits your needs

Investment funds offer access to a range of asset classes, geographical regions and investment techniques. But not all funds perform equally well and picking them takes some careful planning

Why bother? This is the first, and most important, question investors should ask themselves when contemplating the thousands of funds on sale. Not only do the funds vary enormously in quality, but there are also good and bad reasons for investing in one.

A fund is essentially just a basket containing a mix of assets, such as shares, bonds, cash or property. By spreading fixed costs, such as dealing charges, over a wide pool of assets, funds offer investors access to a widely diversified mix of investments in return for a relatively small minimum stake.

So a good reason to buy a fund is to get access to asset classes geographical regions or investment techniques you cannot afford to invest in directly yourself. This does not just apply to exotic areas, such as emerging markets, but to seemingly more mundane investment approaches, such as tracking the UK stockmarket. Very few private investors could afford to run a portfolio of stocks containing all of the 810 companies in the FTSE All-Share index, but you can buy a fund that replicates this index for a fee of just 0.5 per cent a year.

Another reason why many private investors buy a fund is to get exposure to a particular manager's expertise. This rationale is understandable. But bear in mind that star performers can burn out – there is very little correlation between a fund's past performance and its future returns (see 'How the *FT* can help' page 160). What is more, even if you are lucky or prescient enough to find a manager who can consistently outperform the market, he or she may be poached by another fund management group in the future.

While buying a fund on its performance record needs to be done with care, the worst reason to buy a fund is for its tax status. Individual Savings Accounts can be used to hold certain types of funds tax-free – the income paid out by funds held in ISAs is not subject to tax and nor are any profits made by the investor when the fund is sold.

ISAs and their forerunner, Personal Equity Plans, have proved to be a phenomenally successful marketing tool for fund managers. But the tax savings, while welcome, are not always very big – the annual income tax saving for a higher-rate taxpayer on a £6,000 fund with a 3 per cent yield, for instance, is just £72. Even this income tax break is set to be cut for ISAs in 2004, when investors will lose the ability to reclaim basic-rate income tax on dividends from equity-based funds held in the plans.

Do not let the undoubted allure of the tax-free message blind you to the fact that ISAs are nothing more than wrappers for the underlying investments. The performance of those investments will have a far greater effect on your wealth than their tax status – much better a top-quality fund outside a ISA than a dog within it.

How do you assess fund quality and choose one that suits you?

● **What type of fund is best?** This is a case of horses for courses – the question of whether to go for a unit or an investment trust depends partly on what type of assets you want to invest in.

The open-ended nature of unit trusts, which means the fund expands and contracts in response to investor demand, can be a problem in illiquid areas such as emerging markets.

The risk in a severe market fall is that the manager may be forced to sell the best – most easily tradeable – assets in his portfolio to generate cash to meet redemptions. At its most extreme, such as when currency controls were imposed by Malaysia in 1998, trading in open-ended funds may have to be suspended altogether.

But investment trusts have drawbacks too, not least the fact that the share price can fall to a wide discount to the value of the underlying assets. This can be a particular problem in markets that have taken a pounding – the average emerging markets trust was trading on an astonishing 22 per cent discount on 6 November 1998.

Investment trusts, which we discuss in more detail on page 164 can invest in a much wider range of assets and have much greater borrowing powers than unit trusts, because they are structured as companies rather than trusts (see chart, page 156–7).

The line between the two may become more blurred in future. Unit trusts are gradually switching over to a new type of investment structure – open-ended investment companies. These companies, usually referred to by the unattractive acronym OEICs, have a single buying and selling price, as opposed to the bid-offer spread of unit trusts. OEICs also allow managers to hold sub-funds under a single umbrella and to issue different classes of ordinary shares for a fund.

But in most respects, investors who switch from a unit trust to an OEIC will notice little difference – both these types of open-ended funds have much more in common with each other than with the closed-ended investment trusts.

● **Active or passive management?** The debate still rages over whether you are better advised to get a fund designed simply to track a stock market index or one that is actively managed with the aim of beating the market. In practice, most investors are best off with a combination of the two.

The question is which will give you better returns – a cheap fund that tracks a stock market index or one that is actively managed, using stockpicking skills and economic research, to try to outperform it?

Until recently, the evidence was mainly in the trackers' favour. Over the past ten years, only one in five actively managed general UK unit trusts have performed better than the All-Share index.

But the tide has turned against trackers somewhat following the recent market downturn. Some 64 per cent of actively managed funds beat the index over the year to October 1998, according to research by fund manager HSBC Asset Management. Although these figures take no account of the hefty initial charge many active funds levy, the reversal of the performance trend does support active managers' arguments that they can add value by, for example, moving into defensive assets such as cash when markets are volatile.

Index trackers are a very good way of getting exposure to big UK companies. But if you want exposure to smaller UK companies, you

INVESTMENT FUNDS

	unit trust
Nature of fund	Fund size and number of units expand and contract on demand (open-ended)
Legal structure	Trust
Stock Exchange listing	No
Investor's holdings	Units
Capital structure	Can issue only income and accumulation units
Independent board?	No
Assets safeguarded by	Independent trustee
Single price if buying and selling	Not currently, but this will be required by 1 January 2001
Does the price mirror the value of the underlying net assets (NAV)?	Yes, with initial charges reflected in the spread between bid and offer prices
Borrowing powers	Maximum 10 per cent of fund for no more than three months
How often assets are valued	Usually daily
Investment restrictions	Clearly defined rules on what investments the manager may make
Tax	Exempt from tax on capital gains within the fund Income, net of fees and other expenses, subject to corporation tax

Open-ended investment company	Investment trust
Fund size and number of units expand and contract on demand (open-ended)	Fund size and number of units unaffected by demand (closed-ended)
Company with variable capital	Public limited company
Optional	Yes
Shares	Shares
Can issue different classes of ordinary shares	Can issue different classes of shares, including preference shares, and debentures and warrants. Can have a split-capital structure
Optional	Yes
Independent depositary	Custodian (may be part of the management group)
Yes	No
Yes. Charges are shown separately	No. Shares trade at a discount or premium to the NAV
Maximum 10 per cent of fund for no more than three months	Extensive
Usually daily	Usually daily or weekly
Clearly defined rules on what investments the manager may make	Almost unlimited investments allowed, subject to approval by the trust's board
Exempt from tax on capital gains within the company Income, net of fees and other expenses, subject to corporation tax	Exempt from tax on capital gains within the company Income, net of fees and other expenses, subject to corporation tax

need an actively managed fund. Tracking also only works well in big, efficient markets such as the UK and US. In other markets, such as Japan or Asia, active funds have the edge.

● **What is the quality of the management team?** For active funds, investment performance is all important – and extremely hard to predict. The obvious method of looking at the fund's record needs to be used with great caution (see 'How the *FT* can help', page 160).

It is also extremely important to try to get a feel for the quality and approach of the fund's manager and indeed the fund management group as a whole. What is the investment style – top-down or stock-picking, value or growth (see page 64)? What are the research resources? How tightly do individual managers have to conform to the group ethos? How long do the star performers stay?

● **What about costs?** Charges are important for trackers – the higher the fees, the more the fund is likely to underperform its chosen index. These funds should be much cheaper than actively managed funds because they are much easier to run – as a rule of thumb, a tracker should have no initial charges and an annual fee of 1 per cent or less.

For actively managed funds, charges will have less of an effect on your overall return than the investment performance. But the level of costs matters none the less, since the charges act as a drag on performance. The longer you hold the fund – and most unit and investment trusts should be seen as a minimum five-year commitment – the more important the level of the annual fee and the less the effect of the initial charge.

Investment trusts are generally much cheaper than unit trusts. Charges for the latter have crept up in recent years to the point where an annual fee of 1.5 per cent is seen as quite acceptable on top of an initial charge of 3–6 per cent. If you are happy to buy without getting advice, there are ways to cut these costs (see Top Tip, page 162).

ALTERNATIVE INVESTMENTS

Investing overseas

Investors who cannot find what they want from the 2,000 or so unit and investment trusts might be tempted to try one of the 6,200 funds based outside the UK, in centres such as the Channel Islands and Luxembourg. The huge range of offshore funds includes high-risk and esoteric vehicles, designed to appeal to wealthy and sophisticated investors, that would not be allowed under the UK's regulations.

Historically, offshore investments were used mainly by wealthy investors who wanted to defer or avoid certain taxes. But today, virtually all the tax advantages have disappeared for most UK investors.

Many offshore funds reinvest income virtually tax free and can therefore be used by UK investors who want to defer income and capital gains tax. But these funds are not tax-free – when the roll-up fund is cashed in, all the profits you make will be taxed as income.

Offshore funds have other potential drawbacks. The charges are generally higher than their unit or investment trust equivalents, but are often not clearly disclosed. The total annual cost of investing in an offshore fund can be up to four times higher than the quoted management fee, according to a survey published in 1997 by Fitzrovia International. On average, the total cost of an offshore equities fund is almost one percentage point higher than the quoted fee.

Investors also need to keep a watchful eye on the safety of their assets when buying offshore – the level of investor protection may not match that of the UK. Check whether the manager and the custodian firm (which has responsibility for looking after the assets) are regulated. Also ask what, if any, compensation scheme covers investors.

Fund performance

Everyone wants a top-performing fund – but the danger of buying one flagged as such is that this accolade applies to the past and not the future.

The fund performance statistics published in Weekend Money each Saturday are a useful tool for investors, but one that needs to be applied with care. The tables show the top five performing funds in each of the main unit and investment trust sectors, ranked by their total return (capital plus net income) over the past three years.

UNIT TRUSTS

Tables show the result of investing £1,000 over different time periods. Trusts are ranked on 3-ye

■ Europe	1 year (£)	3	5	10	Volatility	Yld%	■ Best P
TU European	1304	2102	-	-	4.6	1.4	TU European
INVESCO European Growth	1365	2068	2789	5312	6.5	-	INVESCO Euro
Newton European	1399	2052	2642	4826	5.7	0.3	Newton Europ
INVESCO European Small Cos	1390	2047	2716	5357	5.7	-	INVESCO Euro
Baring German Growth	1529	1994	2148	-	6.0	0.5	Threadneedle
SECTOR AVERAGE	1188	1638	2016	3970	5.4	0.7	AVERAGE UT
■ Global Emerging Mkts							**■ Prope**
Stewart Ivory Emerging Market	691	876	811	-	7.9	1.5	Norwich Prope
Gartmore PS Emerging Markets	766	827	573	-	8.0	1.4	Aberdeen Proli
Mercury Emerging Markets	651	816	724	-	8.5	0.3	Barclays Prope

These 'top five' will not necessarily be the top five funds over the next three years – in fact, the odds suggest that they almost certainly will not all stay at the top of the league tables.

If a fund is selected at random, there should be a 50 : 50 chance that it will be in the top half of the performance league table for its sector in any given year. Somewhat depressingly, choosing a fund that has achieved above-average performance in the past only slightly increases your odds – to about 57 per cent – that it will achieve above-average performance in the future, according to analysts S&P Fund Research.

This does not mean that you should completely ignore past perform-ance, just that the figures need to be looked at carefully. Do not just look at one time period in isolation. A fund can achieve startlingly good results one year on the back of a high-risk strategy and then plunge to the bottom of the tables the next when the market conditions change.

A consistent performance is what most financial advisers seek – much better a tortoise fund that is steadily above average than a hare that runs out of steam.

One way of judging this is simply to look at performance over a number of periods. The *FT* statistics show the total return over one, three, five and ten years against the sector average, to help you judge whether the trusts shown have been consistently above par.

Another important indicator is the volatility figure (see page 40) quoted for each trust. This measures how much the price fluctuates – the higher the volatility, the greater the fluctuation, which is why the average figure for a high-risk sector such as emerging markets may be double or more that for relatively stable mainstream U K sectors.

For very similar funds in the same sector, the volatility can be a guide to how many risks the manager has taken to achieve the stated perform-ance – the ideal combination for most private investors is a relatively low volatility combined with performance that is consistently well above average.

Remember the need to look behind these figures. Be careful, for example, that you are not buying a fund on the back of the performance of a manager who is no longer running it – more than half of the twenty-five U K unit trusts that have produced the best returns over the past five years no longer have the same manager they had five years ago, according to research by independent advisers Best Investment.

Even if the same manager is still employed by the fund management group, check whether he or she still has a hands-on role running the fund. Good managers can easily get sidetracked into marketing or administration.

Discount brokers

Investors who know which unit trust they want to buy often have to pay exactly the same charges as someone who wants help from an adviser, even if they buy direct from the fund manager. But there is a way round this anomaly. There are a number of specialist discount brokers that offer cut-price deals on individual savings accounts, as well as many unit trusts bought without the ISA wrapper.

The brokers refund all, or part, of the commission paid to advisers, which accounts for most of the initial fee and – in the case of ISAs and a large number of unit trusts – for 0.5 per cent of the annual fee.

The main drawback is that the brokers will not offer deals on all ISAs or unit trusts. Some fund managers, such as Virgin, that do not pay commission are excluded altogether, since there is nothing for the broker to discount. Many brokers also limit their service to lump sum investments of £1,000 or more. If the broker does cover monthly savings schemes, the discount is likely to be a lot less. The best bet is to call a selection of brokers and get quotes. When comparing the deals, do not forget to ask about administration fees. Pep Direct, for example, levies a £25 charge when you invest, so you need to study how this eats into the saving you make on providers' fees.

Note that you will get discounts in different forms, depending on the broker you use. Some will send you a cheque for the value of the discount. Others will use the discount automatically to invest more in the ISA.

Most of the brokers will offer discount deals on a number of other investments, as well as ISAs, including personal pension plans and term assurance.

- **Contacts** There is a wide range of discount brokers, including
  Chelsea Financial Services 0171 351 6022;
  Elson Associates 0500 691790;
  Financial Discounts Direct 01420 549090;
  Garrison Investment 0114 2500720;
  Hargreaves Lansdown 0117 988 9880;
  Individual Saving Accounts Ltd 0115 982 5105;
  Premier Fund Managers 01483 306090;
  Unitas 01724 849481.

Time for another look

The investment trust sector has had a bad run recently. For the past four years, investment trusts have underperformed the UK stock market by about 25 per cent. But the advantages these investments have over unit trusts mean they might be ready for a renaissance

Investment trusts have been the ugly sisters at the fund managers' ball in recent years, standing in the shadows while their unit trust Prince Charming rivals waltz off with investors. But discerning investors looking for a fund would be wise not to ignore investment trusts.

The investment trust sector is undoubtedly in trouble at the moment. While unit trusts have managed to attract more than £20bn of net new money since the start of 1997, investment trusts have lost a net £1.7 bn. Their recent track record helps to explain why the investment trust sector has underperformed the UK stock market by about 25 per cent over the past four years. The record of new trusts is even worse: of the fifty new issues that have raised £50m or more over the past decade, only twenty are making money for their subscribers, while twenty are down by more than 50 per cent, according to analysis by B. T. Alex Brown.

But investment trusts could well bounce back. They have several potential advantages over their unit trust rivals. Investment trusts have independent boards that are meant to protect shareholders' interests (although their degree of success in this respect varies). They have much greater investment flexibility than unit trusts – investment trusts in the venture capital sector, for example, invest mainly in unquoted shares, whereas unit trusts are constrained by their regulations from investing more than 10 per cent of their portfolio in unquoteds.

Investment trusts can gear up by borrowing money to invest. This can be a double-edged sword because in falling markets the gearing will exaggerate the losses. But, provided markets rise more than they fall and the trust gets its timing reasonably right, gearing should enhance long-term returns.

Another important factor is charges. Historically, investment trusts have always been much cheaper than unit trusts. This advantage is being eroded on some of the newer trusts and in the pricing of wrappers such as personal equity plans. None the less, there are some bargains around – the average international general investment trust has total expenses of 0.57 per cent of its assets, according to BT Alex Brown, compared with the annual charge on a typical unit trust of 1.25–1.5 per cent.

So why have investment trusts found it so hard to compete against unit trusts? Part of the answer lies in the fact that trust managers have, until very recently, not paid commissions to independent financial advisers. But for investors who are willing to go it alone, or use a fee-based adviser, the absence of commissions is a positive advantage.

Does this mean the time is ripe to buy into the sector? Fans of investment trusts argue that it is essentially a cyclical sector, so an upturn should be along soon. Cynics argue there is a lot more pain to come before an upturn can even be thought of. As with any type of fund, the answer depends on both the sector you want to invest in and the quality of the fund you get.

But the main points to look for when selecting a trust are:

• **Investment objective.** The broad investment sectors, most of which are listed in the table on page 166, provide a starting point for selecting the type of trust you want. But these are broad parameters only – trusts within the same sector can sometimes have very different investment specializations. If you want to know the trust's investment policy in detail or indeed to get a greater insight into its management philosophy the best bet is to get a copy of the latest annual report and accounts.

• **Discounts.** Unlike unit trusts, where the price of the unit reflects the underlying value of the net assets (NAV), investment trusts usually trade at a discount (or premium) to the NAV. The discount has become the albatross around the sector's neck – the widening of the average discount from 3.5 per cent in January 1994 to about 12 per cent

INVESTMENT TRUSTS

	Risk	Potential return	
		Income	Capital

Conventional trusts

	Risk	Income	Capital
International generalists	Low	Low	Medium
Smaller companies	High	Low	Medium
Income growth	Low	Medium	Medium
High income	High	High	Low
North America	Medium	Low	Medium
Far East excl. Japan	High	Low	High
Far East inc. Japan	High	Low	High
Japan	High	Low	High
Europe	Medium	Low	Medium
Emerging markets	High	Low	High
Venture capital	High	Low	High

Split capital trusts

	Risk	Income	Capital
Zero-dividend preference shares	Low	Nil	Pre-set
Stepped preference shares	Low	Pre-set	Pre-set
Income shares	Varies	High/rising	Various
Ordinary income shares	High	High/rising	Surplus
Capital shares	High	Nil**	Surplus

* A negative sign indicates a premium

** With a few exceptions

† Based on the par, not market, value of the zeros and other securities that have prior right to the assets on redemption

Note that the high/medium/low classifications used for risk, potential returns and discount volatility are generalizations. There are exceptions within each sector.

Performance figures are for a £100 investment, assume net income is reinvested and ignore dealing charges

Figures correct as at 2 November 1998

Source: BT Alex Brown

Five-year performance

Yield per cent	Share price, £	NAV, £	Discount,* per cent
1.9	138	145	14
2.3	101	120	19
3.5	127	141	10
6.0	123	121	-1
0.6	162	184	12
1.1	41	46	20
1.7	62	74	23
Nil	49	54	19
0.9	165	178	12
0.9	55	72	24
2.3	178	192	10
Nil	149	n/a	n/a
4.0	114	n/a	n/a
10.3	70	n/a	n/a
7.1	115	122†	5†
Nil	182	132†	40†

now has been one reason why trusts' share price performance has been so poor.

But discounts can work to investors' advantage, as well as against them. A 20 per cent discount is effectively a way of buying assets for a fifth less than their intrinsic worth although you will be able to realize even part of this hidden value only if the discount subsequently narrows or the trust is wound up (see 'How the *FT* can help', page 171).

Discounts on trusts should not be looked at in isolation. What appears to be a wide discount may be simply the norm for the trust's peer group. There could also be a good reason why a trust is trading on what appears to be an anomalous discount or premium, so check it against the historical average for that particular trust.

● **Investment performance and management quality.** Changes in discount levels are very hard to second-guess. For any investor looking to hold a trust for the medium to long term, the performance of the trust's portfolio – the NAV performance – is generally more important than the share price performance.

As with other funds, the performance figures need to be taken with a fairly hefty pinch of salt. Investors need to try to form their own judgement as to the quality and stability of the trust's manager (see page 153).

● **The trust's board.** The board is there to represent shareholders' interests. So it is worth checking that most of its members are independent of the fund manager, and that some at least appear to have relevant skills and experience.

● **Capital structure.** At its most basic level, this consists of checking the level of quoted debt the trust has issued. But for some trusts, known as split capital trusts, the capital structure needs to be examined extremely carefully.

While conventional investment trusts have been in the doldrums, splits have been undergoing something of a renaissance of late, successfully raising new money and attracting new investors.

Splits are esoteric, often complex, vehicles driven by a deceptively simple idea. Rather than sharing the income and capital growth (or loss) of the trust's portfolio equally between shares, splits issue different types of shares with different capital and income entitlements. Splits have a fixed life, with each class of share having a strictly ordered entitlement to the assets left when the trust is wound up.

In its simplest form, a split cap has income shares, which get all the income from the portfolio but none of the capital growth, and capital shares, which get all the capital growth but none of the income.

This structure means when the capital shares are usually highly geared they magnify stock market rises or falls. In a trust split 50:50 between income and capital shares, for example, the income shares would have double the underlying portfolio yield while the capital shares would have double its gains – or losses.

In practice, most splits have much more complicated structures than this, with a wide range of different share classes, each with a different gearing. The conventional measures used to assess investment trust shares, such as discounts, are irrelevant for many classes of split trust shares. Instead, analysts use measures such as asset cover (the assets available to repay certain classes of share); hurdle rates (the rate of asset growth required to achieve that repayment); and gross redemption yields (the total return that will be achieved on different share classes at different assumed rates of portfolio growth).

The main types of shares issued by split caps, in varying combinations, are:

● **Zero-dividend preference shares.** Zeros, which pay no income, offer a predetermined capital repayment when the trust is wound up. This capital sum is not guaranteed but, because zeros usually rank ahead of other split cap shares in the repayment queue, the shares are relatively low risk. The key points to check with zeros are redemption yield and the level of asset cover.

● **Stepped preference shares.** These shares pay an income which rises at a predetermined rate each year and, like zeros, a predetermined capital repayment when the trust is wound up.

● **Income shares.** Ranking after preference shares, but before capital shares in the repayment queue, income shares generally have very high yields. The capital entitlement varies, ranging from the issue price plus part of any growth of the trust's assets to a purely nominal amount, such as 1p, which in effect guarantees that investors who hold the shares until the trust winds up will lose their original capital.

● **Ordinary income shares.** Also known as income and residual capital shares or highly geared ordinary shares. These offer a high and rising income plus all the assets left over when the trust is wound up after other prior-ranking share classes, such as zeros, have been repaid.

● **Capital shares.** These usually pay no income and rank at the end of the queue for repayment behind other share classes when the trust is wound up, making them a high-risk investment.

Investors who are interested in splits should bear in mind that no two trusts are the same – while some issue the same types of shares, these will generally be in different ratios to each other and have different life-spans. Splits also vary widely in the investment strategy that is adopted, with some having much higher risk portfolios than others. Investors should be confident they understand both a trust's capital structure and its investment strategy before buying shares.

If in any doubt, this is one area where it makes sense to get professional advice.

Future imperfect

Investment trust warrants are relatively common – about 130 trusts have warrants in issue and most new trusts offer subscribers 'free' warrants alongside their shares. But are these investments worth having?

A warrant is in effect a long-term call option – it offers the right to buy shares in the trust at a fixed price (the exercise price) at a fixed date in the future. These terms are set when the warrant is issued. Between issue and expiry, the warrant can be traded just like the shares in the underlying trust.

Warrants magnify the movement of the trust's share price, which makes them risky investments that none the less hold out the prospect of high returns for brave investors.

If warrants are exercised, the trust has to create more shares, which can dilute the net asset value per ordinary share (see 'How the FT can help', page 171). This problem generally arises only if the trust has been successful and the share price has risen sufficiently to make it worthwhile to exercise the warrants. To that extent, investors given 'free' warrants as part of a new share issue lose on the one hand what they gain on the other, in that the more valuable the warrants prove to be, the greater the dilution effect.

In general, investors in new issues have had the opposite problem in recent years. Many new trusts, particularly those investing in the Far East and emerging markets, are now trading at substantially less than their issue price, and their warrants could well expire worthless, without ever having come near to the exercise price.

Factors to look at when assessing a warrant include its life and gearing (the share price divided by the warrant price), as well as the underlying shares' potential for share price growth.

Trust information

The **London share service** gives invaluable daily information on investment trusts. As with other companies, the service shows the **share price** when the stock market closed the day before; **the highest and lowest share price** over the previous year; and the **gross yield**. It also indicates which trusts offer free annual or interim reports through the *FT* **free annual reports club** – a very useful option for prospective investors. The **market capitalization** of each trust is shown in the share service each Monday.

INVESTMENT TRUSTS

	Notes	Price	+ or −	1998 high	low	Yld Gr's	NAV	Dis or Pm(-)
Approved by the Inland Revenue								
3i		535	−3	678	450	2.4	512.4	−4.4
3i Smlr Quoted Co's	†	150½ xd	−½	216	118	3.2	175.3	14.1
AIM Trust		72	......	98½	69½	1.2	92.4	22.1

INV TRUSTS SPLIT CAPITAL

	Notes	Price	+ or −	1998 high	low	Yld Gr's	NAV	Dis or Pm(-)
Approved by the Inland Revenue								
Aberdeen Pfd Zero Dv Pf		227¼	......	229¼	210½	–	–	–
Aberforth Split Inc		72½ xd	......	85	69½	21.2	–	–

The rest of the financial information given differs from that for other companies, reflecting the unique structure of investment trusts. Rather than quoting the p/e ratio, the share service gives an alternative rating for the shares: the **discount** (or premium, shown as a negative figure) between the share price and the underlying **net asset value** (NAV) ascribed to each share.

Discounts are important, but need to be interpreted with a fair degree of caution. For one thing, the basis on which NAVs are calculated can vary – the NAV figures quoted in the *FT*, which are supplied by broker B.T. Alex Brown, are estimated on a daily basis and are 'fully diluted'. This means they assume that, if the trust has warrants in issue with an exercise price that is lower than the NAV, those warrants will be exercised rather than expire worthless. This would dilute the assets available for the ordinary shares. Where a trust has warrants in issue, the share price information gives details immediately following the information on the ordinary shares.

Investors should resist the temptation to assume that the discount represents the amount of value that would be released if the trust were wound up. In practice, investors tend to get back less than this, for two main reasons.

First, the NAV quoted assumes any debt issued by the trust that ranks ahead of the shares will be deducted at its par (nominal) value. In practice, if the trust were wound up, the debt would have to be repaid at its market value, which for many trusts represents a significantly higher cost.

Second, any winding up involves added charges, such as fees to advisers, the costs of cancelling the management contract and the costs of liquidating the portfolio, that are not reflected in the discount.

These two factors can have a substantial impact on the quoted discount. For the sector as a whole, debt accounts for 3 per cent of the assets (excluding venture capital trusts), while the winding-up costs could amount to another 3 per cent, according to estimates by analysts at Merrill Lynch.

The information for **split capital trusts** which is in a separate section immediately after the conventional trusts, follows the same basic format, but the specialized nature of these trusts means that only certain figures are relevant for each share class.

Discounts, for example, are meaningless in relation to zero dividend preference shares because the shares have a predetermined return. The prices of zeros are influenced mainly by interest rates which dictate how attractive that return is to capital-seeking investors rather than the change in the trust's net assets.

Savings schemes

There is a simple, cheap way of buying investment trust shares that many investors are unaware of. Buying through a stockbroker can be prohibitively expensive, particularly for relatively small purchases, because of the high minimum commissions most brokers charge. But most investment trust managers, keen to encourage private investors, now offer savings and investment schemes that can be used to invest either a lump sum or a regular amount each month.

The schemes are generally very cheap, with charges of 1 per cent or less plus the statutory 0.5 per cent stamp duty charge on purchases. Some management groups, such as Edinburgh Fund Managers, Fidelity and Finsbury Asset Management, charge nothing at all, bar stamp duty. The lower costs derive partly from the fact that the scheme managers negotiate cut-price commissions from their broker because they buy and sell shares in bulk, and partly from the fact that trusts sometimes subsidize the scheme to try to attract private investors.

The schemes are usually very flexible, with minimum investments starting as low as £250 for lump sums and £25 for monthly savings, although this varies between managers. Not all trusts, however, are available via the schemes – trusts targeted at institutional investors are often excluded.

Most of the schemes allow you to reinvest dividends for little or no added charge. If you are a monthly saver, the dividend payment will normally be held and added to your next contribution. If you have stopped investing, or are a lump sum investor, the dividends will normally be held until they reach a set minimum amount.

Some schemes also offer a cheap share exchange option, whereby you sell shares in other companies and the proceeds are used to buy shares in the investment trust.

A list of the schemes available, with a brief summary of their charges and features, is given in the free *Guide to Investment Trust Companies* from the Association of Investment Trust Companies (0171 431 5222).

Tax muddies the waters

Some life assurance policies provide nothing but life assurance: you die, they pay. Some are essentially investment or savings schemes with a fig-leaf of life assurance designed to secure the tax concessions life assurance attracts

Life assurance companies also do a lot of other things. For example, they sell unit trusts, pensions and insurance against things such as prolonged disability. This article looks only at their main investment and savings products.

Few people are neutral about life assurance investments. Fans come in two varieties: unsophisticated investors who do not trust stock markets and often do not realize that their money is going near the stock market; and sophisticated ones who often buy them as much for their tax advantages as for their investment performance.

The numerate ones point to the generally good returns produced by many life assurance products. With-profits endowments (see page 176), the traditional backbone of the industry, have recently been producing returns of more than 9 per cent a year in nominal terms (nearly 6 per cent a year after adjusting for inflation).

These are reasonable in themselves, but particularly appealing to higher-rate taxpayers, because they do not have to pay tax on the proceeds.

Foes of life assurance argue that only a minority of investors actually get such high returns; that many customers lose out badly because they inadvertently break the very restrictive terms of life assurance contracts; and that life policies are often sold aggressively to unsuitable customers, partly because of the high commissions they produce for the salesman.

Many also have doctrinal objections to the fuzziness endemic to life assurance. It is very hard for the investor – or any other outsider – to see what is happening to money once it goes into a life company. What is more, life assurance investments may soon be less profitable (see With-profits Policies, page 180).

And what about the underlying investments? As with so many packaged products, the wrapping of life assurance contracts seems to attract more attention than the contents. Broadly all with-profits or unit-linked contracts involve taking a stake in an investment fund. The other products in our table do not involve investment in a fund. The return on them is either predetermined or reflects the performance of an independent stock market index.

Life assurance investments are described as 'policies' and your payments are called 'premiums' because they all provide some life assurance cover as well. But the importance of the assurance element varies. Traditional endowment schemes were conceived as dual-purpose products and include a relatively large amount of life assurance. Newer products, such as maximum investment plans, are essentially investment schemes with a life assurance fig-leaf.

Most advisers argue that life cover bought as part of a package is expensive, and suggest that, if you need some, it is more sensible to buy it separately.

With-profits policies work differently from unit-linked ones.

● **Unit-linked.** Buying a unit-linked policy is a bit like buying a unit trust, but with additional restrictions. You get a reasonable choice of funds and can switch between them. If you do not want to take your own investment decisions, you can choose the managed fund.

The value of your investment is directly linked to the price of the units. And you can follow the price of your units in the daily newspaper.

But there may well be penalties if you want your money back in a hurry. In some cases the company can impose a charge, in others you lose the tax advantages that may well have prompted your decision to buy a life policy rather than a unit trust in the first place.

● **With-profits.** With-profits policies are more complicated. Your money goes into a single managed life fund, usually containing a mixture of shares, bonds, property and cash. But the process for deciding how much of the profits notched up by the fund can be distributed, and which policyholders get what, is pretty arcane and is gradually changing.

The original idea of with-profits funds was that they reduced risk both by spreading it between different investors, and by ironing out the effects of short-term stock market fluctuations over time. Profit allocations are intended to reflect underlying trends, not the position at the date the investor cashes in his policy.

Under a 'conventional' with-profits fund, you are initially guaranteed a basic sum at the end of the investment term (maturity) and this is augmented by the profits earmarked for your policy each year as an annual 'bonus'. Once allocated to your policy, bonuses cannot be taken away, although the rate for future years is not guaranteed.

In addition to the annual bonus, the insurance company pays a final or 'terminal' bonus at the end of your investment period (or when you die, if earlier). Note though that this bonus is discretionary and tends to reflect recent performance.

In recent years, companies have watered down the guarantees on traditional with-profits policies by switching the emphasis from the annual bonus to the discretionary terminal bonus.

Also, most companies have switched to a 'unitized' with-profits policy, which does not have a basic sum guaranteed at maturity. Bonuses are reinvested each year, but a clause in the contract, the 'market value adjustment', means the company can reduce the value of your units if you want to get out when there is a run on funds – after a market crash, for example.

Some advisers say investors should think hard before taking out a life assurance contract: the mechanics are obscure and the contract is inflexible. They are popular because investors who have stuck to the contract terms and benefited from the tax breaks have often done very well in the past. But actuaries are now warning that policyholders, like other investors, should lower their expectations.

BLUFFER'S GUIDE TO LIFE ASSURANCE INVESTMENTS

Life company

Others

With-profits

Guaranteed-income bond
Type
Lump sum for 1–5 year period with fixed interest rate
Advantages
* Competitive rates
* Higher-rate taxpayers benefit
Disadvantages
* Inflexible
* Unsuitable for non-taxpayers
Risk rating
Low
Taxation
Basic-rate tax deducted. Higher-rate tax liability. Non-taxpayers cannot reclaim
Possible customers
Cautious income investors
Alternatives
* Some National Savings products, gilts, deposits

Stock market guaranteed bond
Type
Lump sum (typically five years)
Advantages
Guarantees minimum capital sum at end of investment period plus proportion of rise in stock market index
Disadvantages
* Inflexible
* Penalties on early surrender
* Less potential than shares
Taxation
As for guaranteed-income bonds
Possible customers
Cautious equity investors
Alternatives
Protected unit trusts

High-income bonds
Type
Lump sum
Advantages
High income and some capital growth if relevant stock market(s) achieve(s) target growth
Disadvantages
No capital protection
Risk rating
Usually very high
Taxation
As for guaranteed-income bonds
Possible customers
* Unsuitable for most people
* Aimed at income-hungry investors unaware of/willing to accept the high risks
Alternatives
* Some corporate bonds and gilts, annuities

With-profits endowments
Type
Regular payments for ten+ years
Advantages
* Less volatile than stock market
* Progressive capital guarantees
* Higher-rate taxpayers benefit
Disadvantages
* Opaque
* Inflexible
* Poor value if cashed in early
* Not suitable for non-taxpayers
Risk rating
Low
Taxation
Fund pays equivelent of basic rate tax. Non-taxpayers cannot reclaim; higher-rate taxpayers normally exempt from additional tax liability
Possible customers
Cautious higher-rate taxpayers
Alternatives
* Regular savings in unit trusts, OEICS

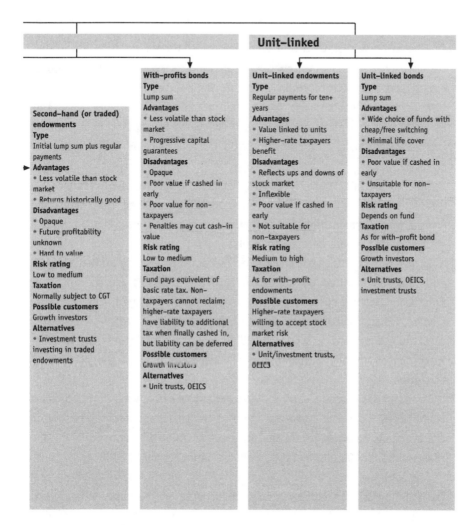

Unit-linked

Second-hand (or traded) endowments
Type
Initial lump sum plus regular payments
► **Advantages**
• Less volatile than stock market
• Returns historically good
Disadvantages
• Opaque
• Future profitability unknown
• Hard to value
Risk rating
Low to medium
Taxation
Normally subject to CGT
Possible customers
Growth investors
Alternatives
• Investment trusts investing in traded endowments

With-profits bonds
Type
Lump sum
Advantages
• Less volatile than stock market
• Progressive capital guarantees
Disadvantages
• Opaque
• Poor value if cashed in early
• Poor value for non-taxpayers
• Penalties may cut cash-in value
Risk rating
Low to medium
Taxation
Fund pays equivelent of basic rate tax. Non-taxpayers cannot reclaim; higher-rate taxpayers have liability to additional tax when finally cashed in, but liability can be deferred
Possible customers
Growth investors
Alternatives
• Unit trusts, OEICS

Unit-linked endowments
Type
Regular payments for ten+ years
Advantages
• Value linked to units
• Higher-rate taxpayers benefit
Disadvantages
• Reflects ups and downs of stock market
• Inflexible
• Poor value if cashed in early
• Not suitable for non-taxpayers
Risk rating
Medium to high
Taxation
As for with-profit endowments
Possible customers
Higher-rate taxpayers willing to accept stock market risk
Alternatives
• Unit/investment trusts, OEICS

Unit-linked bonds
Type
Lump sum
Advantages
• Wide choice of funds with cheap/free switching
• Minimal life cover
Disadvantages
• Poor value if cashed in early
• Unsuitable for non-taxpayers
Risk rating
Depends on fund
Taxation
As for with-profit bond
Possible customers
Growth investors
Alternatives
• Unit trusts, OEICS, investment trusts

WITH-PROFIT POLICIES

Bonus payments

The actuarial art of with-profits bonus calculation and distribution has always been a mystery. However, it is possible to identify trends in annual bonus rates and the total returns on maturing policies.

Whereas terminal bonuses (paid when a policy matures) are backwards looking, annual bonuses are fixed with an eye to future prospects, notably interest-rate trends. But companies do not always read those prospects correctly.

Thus, in the late 1980s, when interest rates and investment returns were unusually high, optimism ruled: the companies assumed that rates and returns would remain high. So annual bonus payments were kept at what – with hindsight – were unrealistic levels.

By the early 1990s, most companies had started reducing annual bonuses and they have carried on doing so. Now the actuaries are warning that annual bonuses will continue to fall, because of the change in the economic climate, which is cutting investment returns generally: inflation and interest rates are low by historic standards. What is more, total returns will increasingly depend on the terminal bonus – which is paid at the companies' discretion.

The actuaries recently warned that total payouts from with-profits policies could fall by 7 per cent a year for the next ten years, assuming no change in the economic background. So the proceeds of an investment similar to one that produced £100,000 in 1998 might be only £50,000 in 2008.

The actuaries emphasize that policyholders should concentrate on real (inflation-adjusted) returns: these could drop to perhaps 3 per cent, compared with historic levels of around 6 per cent. But those from different companies will vary.

Life bonds

The *FT*'s weekly **best deposit rates table** always includes a section on the best rates available on fixed-rate guaranteed income life bonds for various deposit periods. The rates on offer are often relatively attractive to higher-rate taxpayers, because of a tax quirk.

■ Best deposit rates

Always remember to consider your own tax status when deciding which is the best for you. One feature of our savings rates tables is best rates for the second generation of Tessas. If you have a maturing Tessa, you have up to six months to decide whether to reinvest your capital for a further five years in a new Tessa. The table lists some of the best rates currently available for "Tessa Twos".

Instant Access Accounts	Telephone	Account	Notice or term	Deposit	Rate	Interest paid
Northern Rock(Gnsy) Ltd	01481 718121	Offshore 90 Day	90 Day	£25,000	8.00%	Yly
Guaranteed Income bonds (net)						
NPI	01222 782360		13.12.99	£10,000	5.63%FN	Yly
AIG Life (UK)	0700 244 5433		2 Yr	£5,000	4.60%FN	Yly
AIG Life (UK)	0700 244 5433		3 Yr	£5,000	4.60%FN	Yly
AIG Life (UK)	0700 244 5433		4 Yr	£5,000	4.00%FN	Yly
Wesleyan Assurance	0800 2288557		5 Yr	£10,000	5.50%FN	Mly
National Savings accounts & bonds (gross)			Notice or term	Deposit	Rate %	Interest paid
INVESTMENT ACCOUNTS			1 Month	£20	5.00%	Yly
				£500	5.25%	Yly
				£2,500	5.50%	Yly
				£5,000	5.75%	Yly
				£10,000	6.00%	Yly
				£25,000	6.25%	Yly

The interest on the bonds is paid out net of basic-rate tax (see below), and the tax cannot be reclaimed by people not liable to tax. So they are generally bad value for low- and non-taxpayers. For basic-rate taxpayers, the rates on the bonds can be directly compared with those on any other investment, on either a net or gross basis. If, say, a bond has a net return of 5.5 per cent a year, the gross equivalent to a basic-rate taxpayer would be 6.875 per cent. So they are only worth considering if that is better than other rates available.

But higher-rate taxpayers have to pay only 17 per cent additional tax on income from insurance bonds, compared with 20 per cent on income from other savings and investments. What is more, this 17 per cent is levied on the net income paid out to them, not on a notional gross figure.

All very abstruse. But what it comes down to in practice is that a payment from an insurance bond is worth roughly a tenth more to a higher-rate taxpayer than a similar payment from a bank or building society.

In our example of a 5.5 per cent payment, the return to the higher-rate taxpayer after his additional tax payment is 4.565 per cent, equivalent to a gross rate of 7.6 per cent. On a similar payout from a bank or building society deposit, the comparable figures are 4.125 per cent and 6.875 per cent.

Some life companies have recently started issuing a new type of variable-rate bond, with much higher interest rates than the fixed ones. They have the same tax advantages for higher-rate taxpayers and can provide a good alternative to high-interest accounts or cash unit trusts.

Why should life company bonds have this unfair advantage? It is just one element in the companies' Byzantine tax structure.

● Life assurance products are sometimes described as tax free: in fact all life products have corporation tax deducted (at 23 per cent) on capital gains and income before the proceeds are paid out. This covers an investor's liability to basic-rate income tax. But the tax cannot be reclaimed. So life products are usually unsuitable for non-taxpayers. They also give investors no chance to make use of their annual capital-gains tax allowance.

● Some policies are classed as qualifying policies, with the consequence that no additional tax is payable even by higher-rate taxpayers. Essentially only policies involving regular payments for ten or more years, with a minimum amount of life cover, qualify.

● Other concessions mean that, even if higher-rate taxpayers invest in non-qualifying policies, they may still be able to defer or even avoid tax in some circumstances.

● The Inland Revenue's stated intention of closing any remaining tax loopholes could hurt investors with over-complicated products, particularly those involving offshore trusts.

Don't surrender

An estimated 70 per cent of endowment policies never make it to maturity, but are cashed in by investors early – a process known as 'surrendering'. Do not do it.

Policies surrendered early seldom provide a good return on your investment. This is mainly because a high proportion of the cost of selling the policy is deducted during the first few years.

So what should you do, if you already have an endowment policy, but really cannot afford to maintain contributions? There are three other ways of making the best of an unwanted endowment contract. Freeze it, borrow against it, or sell it. Sadly but inevitably, all are most effective if the policy has already run long enough to acquire substantial value. Policies often have no value in their early years: all your premiums have been swallowed up in charges. So start with a sighting shot: ask the company what the surrender value of your policy is.

If it is worth a reasonable sum, you can make the policy 'paid up', which means you no longer pay premiums but leave the money sitting in the fund until the maturity date. This allows you to benefit from growth in the underlying investments. But, before you take this step, check whether the level of ongoing charges is unacceptably high.

If you need the capital, most insurance companies offer a cheap loan based on the surrender value of your policy.

Alternatively you might be able to get 15–30 per cent more than the surrender value by selling the policy in the secondhand market.

In this case, an investor buys the policy from you and takes over the commitment to pay the regular premiums. In return the investor is entitled to the entire payout when the policy matures or when you die, whichever is earlier.

The two main options here are to auction the policy, or to sell it to a market maker.

A few companies reckon that their surrender values are better than the secondhand values. But always check the alternatives before accepting the company's offer.

Your most important investment
When you retire, your pension fund should be one of the most valuable things you own

When it comes to pensions you need to set your sights high. By the time you retire, your pension fund should be one of your two most valuable assets. (The other is your home.)

The reason we need such large pension funds is simple. As a nation we are living longer yet retiring earlier. But the welfare state provides nothing more than a subsistence level of benefits.

The key to a financially healthy retirement is to start your pension plan early and to save at a rate that will provide you with an appropriate pension for life. Company schemes usually have a fixed rate of employee contribution of 5 per cent of salary, but there is scope to top up if you start late.

Those who start a personal pension in their early thirties should contribute about 10 per cent of annual earnings, but if you do not start until you are forty you might need to put in as much as 20 per cent. If you are lucky your employer will help you meet the cost.

But some schemes produce more reliable benefits or better results than others. The factors that affect the outcome vary. In a traditional salary-related company scheme the fund managers make all the investment decisions. If the performance is lower than expected your employer is obliged by law to make good any shortfall.

However, if you are responsible for your own plan you need to consider which assets make appropriate long-term investments and shop around for the best fund management and administration.

Company schemes take a very long-term view and typically invest about 80 per cent in UK and overseas equities, with the rest in UK and overseas bonds, cash and sometimes a small percentage in property.

Younger people with a personal plan are usually advised to invest 100 per cent in equities until about ten years before their expected retirement date, at which point it is time to consider switching gradually into assets that safeguard your capital, such as gilts and cash (see page 35). Our chart helps you pick the most suitable type of scheme.

Now down to the mechanics. A pension scheme or plan is not an investment in its own right but a tax-efficient wrapper in which you hold assets. The aims of the pension fund are to provide you with a (taxable) retirement income and a tax-free lump sum.

Good company schemes also provide dependants' pensions if you die, plus a disability pension if you are too ill to work. People with personal pensions have to buy this kind of protection separately.

You qualify for full tax relief on your contributions to a pension arrangement approved by the Inland Revenue, and the pension fund itself grows virtually tax-free.

There are three sources of pension: the state scheme; company schemes; and private plans, the most common of which is the personal pension.

● **State pension.** Do not rely on the state pension – it is constantly under review and there is nothing rock solid about the eligibility rules.

The maximum basic state pension is £66.75 per week since April 1999, while the maximum state earnings related pension (SERP) is just over £100. Eligibility for the benefit depends on your national insurance contributions (NICs) and, possibly, on the contributions of your spouse.

Many employees 'contract out' of SERP through a company or personal pension scheme: part of your NICs are redirected into your private scheme to provide a replacement pension. The self-employed cannot belong to SERP.

● **Company (occupational) schemes.** If your employer offers a pension scheme you should generally join it: in many cases the benefits are guaranteed and your employer will make a substantial contribution on your behalf.

If there is no company scheme there may be a group or 'industry-wide' pension organized by your trade union or professional body. This is likely to offer better value than an individual personal pension due to economies of scale.

A final salary or 'defined benefit' company scheme links your pension to your salary – usually averaged over the last three years before retirement. The maximum pension is two-thirds of final salary, generally after 40 years of service.

With a final salary scheme, there is no direct link between the amount you pay in, the investment performance of the fund and what you get out. Your employer must contribute whatever is necessary to keep the fund solvent.

You can pay up to 15 per cent of annual earnings to a company scheme, but a typical scheme would expect you to pay about 5 per cent, deducted monthly from your pay cheque.

Unless you contribute the maximum to the company scheme, you can top up your pension by paying into the company's 'additional voluntary contributions' (AVC) scheme. Alternatively, you can invest in some other suitable tax-efficient investment.

The second type of company pension scheme is known as **money purchase** or 'defined contribution'. This is increasingly popular with companies.

With a money purchase scheme, your employer does not guarantee you a certain level of pension. Instead, the company simply decides how much it will contribute, and leaves it to its employees to check whether there will be enough in the fund to pay for a decent pension when they retire.

Under the most common money purchase scheme – a group personal pension – the maximum total contribution for you and your employer combined starts at 17.5 per cent of annual earnings up to age thirty-five, rising to 40 per cent for the over sixties. The maximum salary on which contributions can be based is £90,600 (1999–2000).

As a very rough guide you will need total employee–employer contributions of about 10 per cent throughout your working life to build up a decent-sized fund. Clearly if you are a late starter you will need to put in much more than this.

Under any money purchase scheme or plan (including personal

WHICH IS THE RIGHT PENSION FOR YOU?

188

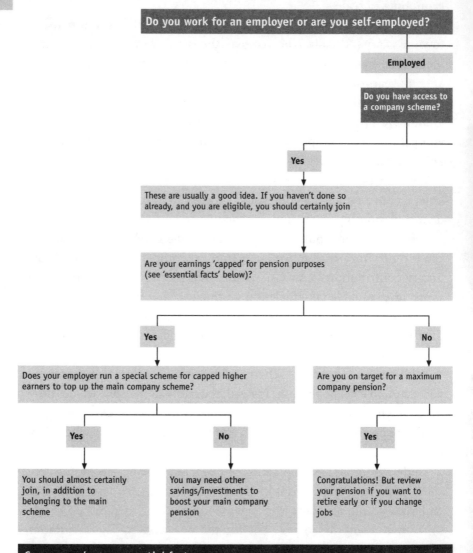

Do you work for an employer or are you self-employed?

Employed

Do you have access to a company scheme?

Yes

These are usually a good idea. If you haven't done so already, and you are eligible, you should certainly join

Are your earnings 'capped' for pension purposes (see 'essential facts' below)?

Yes — **No**

Does your employer run a special scheme for capped higher earners to top up the main company scheme?

Are you on target for a maximum company pension?

Yes — **No** — **Yes**

You should almost certainly join, in addition to belonging to the main scheme

You may need other savings/investments to boost your main company pension

Congratulations! But review your pension if you want to retire early or if you change jobs

---

Company schemes: essential facts
- Your contributions are tax–free, the fund grows largely free of tax, but the pension itself is taxed as income although you can take a tax-free cash lump sum
- Company schemes also offer important dependants' benefits
- Maximum employee contribution 15 per cent of earnings. Employer also contributes
- Certain high earners are 'capped' which means that the maximum salary that can be taken into account for contributions and benefits is £87,600 in 1998/99
- Normal retirement date typically is sixty–five. If you go early your pension will be reduced
- Most schemes link pension to final salary, but growing minority build up fund you use to buy annuity at retirement. Annuity pays a regular guaranteed income

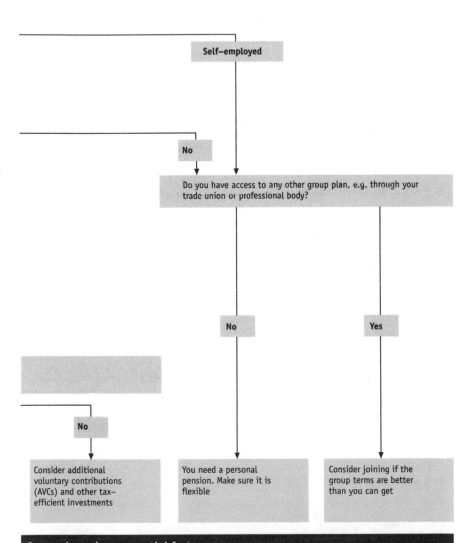

Self-employed

No

Do you have access to any other group plan, e.g. through your trade union or professional body?

No   **Yes**

No

Consider additional voluntary contributions (AVCs) and other tax-efficient investments

You need a personal pension. Make sure it is flexible

Consider joining if the group terms are better than you can get

Personal pensions: essential facts
- You can take out a personal pension if you are self-employed, in a partnership, or employed but not in a company scheme
- Similar tax breaks as for company schemes
- If you die, your spouse wil only get back the fund value
- Your employer can contribute to your personal pension but is not obliged to do so
- Maximum combined employee/employer contribution starts at 17.5 per cent rising to 40 per cent
- Maximum earnings on which contributions can be based are £87,600 (1998/99)
- You can take your pension from a personal plan at any time between age fifty and seventy-five
  Up to 25 per cent of the fund as tax-free cash, with rest used to buy annuity

pensions) your retirement income will depend on four factors: the level of contributions paid by the employee and employer; the performance of the fund; the charges the pension company deducts from your contributions before they are invested; and annuity rates at the time you retire.

At retirement your fund is used to buy an annuity from an insurance company, which provides the regular retirement income, guaranteed for life. The level of income, or annuity 'rate', will depend partly on the size of your fund and partly on yields on gilts – the investments insurance companies buy to generate the income stream. Gilt yields vary a lot from year to year, which makes the conversion from pension fund to annuity a bit of a lottery.

● **Personal pensions.** Personal pensions operate in a similar way to group money purchase schemes. So your retirement income depends on the factors set out above, although charges will be higher on an individual plan. Your employer may contribute within the maximum limits mentioned above but is not obliged to do so.

HIGHER-PAID EMPLOYEES

Pension capping

A growing number of higher-paid employees need to arrange a supplementary pension, because their main one will be lower than they might expect, because they are not allowed to base it on their entire salary. The maximum salary on which their pension contributions and benefits can be based is £90,600 a year (in 1999–2000), a restriction known as the 'earnings cap'. So, even if they earn twice that – £175,000 a year – their company pension will still be based on £87,600.

Who is affected? The cap, which rises broadly in line with inflation every year, applies to members of final salary schemes set up after the 1989 Budget and members who joined any final salary scheme after 1 June 1989. For these employees the maximum contribution for the 1999–2000 tax year is £13,590 and the maximum pension £60,400.

Two types of pension are designed to cater for earnings above the cap: a funded 'unapproved' retirement benefit scheme, and the unfunded equivalent, under which your employer agrees to pay a benefit out of the company's own funds when you retire. The former is arguably more secure because there is a specific fund set up under trust for you and your dependants.

'Unapproved' means that, although the schemes are recognized by the Inland Revenue as genuine pension arrangements, they do not receive the same favourable tax treatment as the 'approved' schemes discussed elsewhere in this section.

Employers are under no obligation to provide a scheme for capped employees. So it is up to you to ask for one or to negotiate extra salary to compensate for the loss of pension rights. And remember, changing jobs could put you into the capped classes.

HOW THE FT CAN HELP

Annuity rates

An annuity provides a guaranteed (taxable) income for life in return for a lump sum investment. And anyone with a personal pension or money purchase group pension scheme has to use his accumulated pension fund to buy an annuity when he retires. (Only people with final salary schemes are exempt.)

The purchase is one of the most important financial decisions people make, because it determines their main income for the rest of their life. Weekend Money publishes tables highlighting the **top annuity rates** every weekend.

The year 1998 was a nightmare for many people because stock market movements meant both that the value of their pension fund had fallen and that the value of the annuity they can buy with a given lump sum had also fallen. Result: their pension is considerably smaller than they expected. Although stock markets have recovered, annuity rates remain low.

The actual annuity 'rate' – or level of income per £1,000 you invest – will depend on your life expectancy and gilt yields. You have no obligation to buy your annuity from your pension company, so shop around with the help of an independent financial adviser. However, check first if your pension company applies a penalty if you leave or, more craftily, a 'loyalty bonus' if you stay put.

■ Top annuity rates

An annuity provides a guaranteed income for life in return for a lump sum investment. The bulk of the fund built up by many types of pension plan must be used in this way. Annuity income is fully taxable. This week's table shows the best rates for PERSONAL PENSION ANNUITIES which are used for personal pension plans and the previous retirement annuity contracts. The rates in the chart do not include inflation proofing.

Male age 55	Annuity +2.63%	Female age 50	Annuity +4.69%
Stalwart Ass	£5,557.00	Canada Life	£4,938.60
Canada Life	£5,509.32	Prudential	£4,716.72
Sun Life	£5,440.80	Stalwart Ass	£4,679.00
Male age 60	**Annuity +1.90%**	**Female age 60**	**Annuity +4.26%**
Stalwart Ass	£6,153.00	Canada Life	£5,707.80
Sun Life	£6,094.80	Stalwart Ass	£5,527.00
Canada Life	£6,062.76	Sun Life	£5,428.92
Male age 70	**Annuity +1.28%**	**Female age 70**	**Annuity +9.25%**

Different types of pension scheme have different rules and require different annuities. So Weekend Money publishes a different table each week on a rolling four-week basis to show what you can get for a fund worth £100,000. We also include figures for 'joint life' annuities which continue to pay your pension to your spouse if you die first. We cover:

● **Personal pension annuity rates,** exclusive of an inflation link. These are offered to investors with a personal pension plan and/or its predecessor, a retirement annuity plan. If you want an inflation link, the rate will be lower.

● **Compulsory purchase annuity rates,** exclusive of an inflation link. These are offered to members of group money purchase schemes. AVC schemes and FSAVC plans.

● **Compulsory purchase annuity rates,** inclusive of a 5 per cent annual inflation link. As above.

● **Purchased life annuity rates.** Anyone can buy a PLA with spare capital if they want a guaranteed income. Rates can be attractive for those over seventy and, unlike pension annuities, the PLA income is not fully taxable.

You may be able to obtain better rates if you have access to an affinity group insurance company, such as the RNPFN for health service employees and their families. Special rates are also available to those in ill health as their life expectancy may be shorter than average.

All of the annuities in the *FT* tables offer a simple exchange: you hand over your fund and secure your income. It is possible to defer converting your pension fund into an annuity in a single transaction. A more flexible arrangement may be attractive if you plan to work part time in early retirement or you think that annuity rates are very poor.

'Income drawdown' and 'phased retirement' plans allow you to draw a flexible income and keep the rest of your fund fully invested, but they are complicated, expensive and risky. Only for the affluent.

TOP TIP

How to avoid risk

If you ever get a chance to join a final salary pension scheme, take it – unless there are obvious reasons why it is unsuitable for you. Final salary schemes leave the employer with all the investment risk: if the investments do worse than expected, the employer has to cough up the difference in order to produce the pension promised. Money purchase schemes leave the risk with the employee: if the investments do worse than expected, the employee gets a smaller pension.

So an employee in a money purchase scheme needs to understand and manage this risk and know what his fund should be invested in.

At the high-risk end of the spectrum is the decision to select funds that keep you fully invested in equities right up to, and even into, retirement. This is fine if you will have other sources of income, but if your pension plan is your only or main source you should protect yourself against volatile equity markets as you approach retirement.

The three main methods of risk management currently available are lifestyle programmes, the use of derivative funds, and with-profits funds. All aim to shield the investor from a fall in the stock markets shortly before retirement, but the mechanics are different.

A lifestyle programme, offered by most group schemes and individual pension companies, automatically switches you from equities into gilts and cash during the ten years leading up to retirement. The downside here is that you come out of equities comparatively early on. Moreover, the basic lifestyle model does not cope well with unplanned early retirement.

As an alternative, some funds use derivatives to insure against a fall in the stock markets. These can work well in the short term, but over the long term they are expensive. Also, derivative-backed funds generally forfeit equity dividends, which provide a substantial element in the total return.

The mechanics and defects of different types of with-profits funds are explained on pages 176–7.

Annuity An annuity provides a guaranteed income for life in return for a lump sum payment. Often bought with a pension fund on retirement. Annuity rates are linked to yields on gilt-edged securities.

Assets That which a company owns, as against liabilities, which it owes. Assets are divided into fixed assets (such as buildings or machinery) and current assets (such as trading stock, cash and investments). Net current assets are current assets minus current liabilities.

Bond Tradeable certificate of debt issued by a government or a company. Always guarantees regular payment of interest; usually guarantees repayment of capital on a specified future date.

Closed-end investment funds Investment funds with a fixed share capital. Open-ended funds grow or shrink according to investor demand.

Concentrated/lop-sided portfolio Portfolio containing only a few shares, or shares in the same industry.

Correlation (with other assets) Movement in the same direction at the same time.

Cyclical A cyclical company's profits ebb and flow with economic cycles.

Discount rate The rate of interest used to express a stream of future income in today's money values: £100 due to be received in ten years' time is less valuable than £100 tomorrow – provided interest rates are positive.

Discounted value Present value of the future sum after it has been discounted back. The higher the discount rate used, the lower the present value of the future sum.

Dividend cover A company's annual earnings per share divided by its annual dividend.

Drawdown Income drawdown pension schemes allow people to defer buying an annuity when they retire and instead draw an income directly from the fund.

Equity income fund A fund investing in high-yielding equities in order to pay above-average dividends. Capital growth is not a priority.

Exchange control risk The danger that a government may hamper or stop the flow of money in and out of a country, as in Malaysia in 1998.

Fledgling index Charts the stock market performance of the 800 or so quoted companies too small to be included in the All-Share index.

Franchise (as in 'strong consumer franchise') Some companies with strong brand recognition, such as Coca-Cola or Gillette, can charge more than 'cost plus' without harming sales.

'Free' cashflow Starts with EBITDA (earnings before interest, tax depreciation and amortization) and deducts the tax paid and, usually, capital expenditure.

Gearing Also called leverage. Situation where small changes in underlying conditions produce big swings in profits. Gearing can be financial – as in futures and options, or in companies with large borrowings – or operational – as in companies with large fixed overheads.

Gilt strips The government equivalent of zero-dividend bonds. The return comes as capital gain.

Leverage The same as gearing.

Liquidity A share is liquid when it is easy to buy or sell without moving the price. The same applies to markets.

Margins Profit margin is trading profit as a percentage of sales. Trading profit reflects the underlying profitability of the business, not whether the company is making money for shareholders. It is calculated before interest charges and tax.

Market capitalization Market value of the equity of a company at the current market price (number of shares in issue multiplied by the share price). Market cap plus the market value of a company's debt is known as the enterprise value.

Nominal return Return that does not take account of the effect of inflation.

Non-financials index The FTSE All-Share index, excluding financial companies and investment trusts.

OEICS Open-ended investment companies – a new-fangled substitute for unit trusts, with a single price for buying and selling.

Options/futures An option is the right but not the obligation to buy or sell a security at a present price. Futures are contracts to buy or sell standardized amounts of a commodity or financial instrument – such as a share or index – at a specific date in the future.

Portfolio Collection of investments, normally consisting of shares, fixed interest stocks and cash. Good portfolios have an objective, and the selection of investments is designed to achieve it.

Price/earnings ratio Relates the current share price to the amount per share earned or expected to be earned by a company.

Protected funds Funds with limited vulnerability to market setbacks.

Recovery shares Companies that have fallen on hard times but could bounce back.

Risk premium Discount rates used for risky assets, such as equities, are higher than those used for risk-free assets, such as gilts. Equity risk premium is the difference.

Share buy-back In some circumstances it can make sense for companies to buy in their own shares. Provided the price is right, earnings per share on the remaining shares should rise. And some financiers argue that as long as debt is cheaper than equity, managements ought to replace equity with debt, even if it risky.

SmallCap index Charts performance of the 500 or so smaller quoted companies in the All-Share index, i.e. those below the top 350 companies.

Split-capital trusts Investment trusts with more than one class of capital – such as income and growth shares.

Yield The annual rate of income on a share or bond that an investor would earn from the security at the current market price.

PENGUIN ONLINE

READ MORE IN PENGUIN

In every corner of the world, on every subject under the sun, Penguin represents quality and variety – the very best in publishing today.

For complete information about books available from Penguin – including Puffins, Penguin Classics and Arkana – and how to order them, write to us at the appropriate address below. Please note that for copyright reasons the selection of books varies from country to country.

In the United Kingdom: Please write to *Dept. EP, Penguin Books Ltd, Bath Road, Harmondsworth, West Drayton, Middlesex UB7 0DA*

In the United States: Please write to *Consumer Sales, Penguin Putnam Inc., P.O. Box 12289 Dept. B, Newark, New Jersey 07101-5289*. VISA and MasterCard holders call 1-800-788-6262 to order Penguin titles

In Canada: Please write to *Penguin Books Canada Ltd, 10 Alcorn Avenue, Suite 300, Toronto, Ontario M4V 3B2*

In Australia: Please write to *Penguin Books Australia Ltd, P.O. Box 257, Ringwood, Victoria 3134*

In New Zealand: Please write to *Penguin Books (NZ) Ltd, Private Bag 102902, North Shore Mail Centre, Auckland 10*

In India: Please write to *Penguin Books India Pvt Ltd, 11 Community Centre, Panchsheel Park, New Delhi 110017*

In the Netherlands: Please write to *Penguin Books Netherlands bv, Postbus 3507, NL-1001 AH Amsterdam*

In Germany: Please write to *Penguin Books Deutschland GmbH, Metzlerstrasse 26, 60594 Frankfurt am Main*

In Spain: Please write to *Penguin Books S. A., Bravo Murillo 19, 1° B, 28015 Madrid*

In Italy: Please write to *Penguin Italia s.r.l., Via Benedetto Croce 2, 20094 Corsico, Milano*

In France: Please write to *Penguin France, Le Carré Wilson, 62 rue Benjamin Baillaud, 31500 Toulouse*

In Japan: Please write to *Penguin Books Japan Ltd, Kaneko Building, 2-3-25 Koraku, Bunkyo-Ku, Tokyo 112*

In South Africa: Please write to *Penguin Books South Africa (Pty) Ltd, Private Bag X14, Parkview, 2122 Johannesburg*

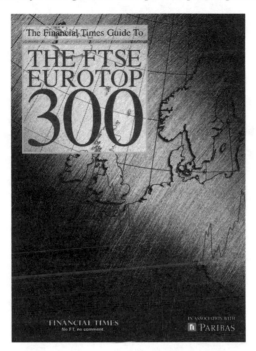

FT Cityline

Fast, convenient access to the City's latest share price information.

All our services are available via telephone and fax-back 24 hours a day.

For a free user directory call the **FT Cityline Help Desk** on +44 171 873 4378 or email us at **Cityline@ft.com**

Alternatively details on how to use the service can be found on the London Share Service pages of the FT newspaper each Monday.

All access to and use of FT Cityline is subject to our terms and conditions, details of which can be provided on request.

FINANCIAL TIMES
No FT, no comment.